BEST *of the* BEST

PRESENTS

Not Just for Diabetics
Cookbook

Naturally Delicious Recipes
for Optimum Wellness

BEST *of the* BEST

PRESENTS

Not Just for Diabetics
Cookbook

Naturally Delicious Recipes
for Optimum Wellness

Dr. James Rouse

with Dr. Debra Rouse

Wellness Experts and Founders of Optimum Wellness™

QUAIL RIDGE PRESS
Preserving America's Food Heritage

ISBN–13: 978–1-934193-81-5
ISBN–10: 1-934193-81-X

On the front cover: Arugula Salad with Scallops and Basil (page 83), Fancy Grilled Cheese (page 135), Chorizo Stuffed Mini Peppers (page 27), and Carrot Zucchini Cake with Whipped Cream Frosting (page 183).

On the back cover: Smoked Salmon Quiche (page 63), Baby Bok Choy Salad (page 87), Mock Milkshake (page 13), Turkey Cranberry Wrap (page 147), and Stuffed Red Bell Peppers (page 115).

Photos by Debra Rouse • Design by Cynthia Clark

Printed in the United States of America

First edition, June 2012

Disclaimer: This book offers healthy recipes, including food and beverages, and tips that should be enjoyed as part of an overall healthy diet and lifestyle and is not intended as a dietary prescription. Persons with health concerns should seek the advice of a qualified healthcare professional, such as a physician or registered dietitian, for a personalized diet plan.

QUAIL RIDGE PRESS
P. O. Box 123 • Brandon, MS 39043
info@quailridge.com • www.quailridge.com

Contents

Drs. James and Debra Rouse

Introduction

This cookbook is a call to action, an opportunity to take a stand for loving self care—affirmative living and eating. The time is right for a revolution. We can come together over good food, and nourish our minds, our bodies, and our spirits. You have the desire, and we have the recipes. The choice to embrace and embark on a journey towards optimum wellness is achieved one meal, one thought, and one empowering choice at a time. First open your mind, and then open your mouth, and savor a lifestyle that is fun, delicious and affirmative.

We love food. We enjoy creating recipes, testing them out on our family, friends, and our patients. We met in pre-med, and we were drawn together both by our interest in medicine and science, as well as our love of living well. We learned about the healing power of food while studying medicine. We practiced and witnessed its power while we partnered with a friend in running and cooking at our restaurant, the Common Sense Cafe in Portland, Oregon. Over the last twenty years, Debra and I have created our own fit kitchen at home. We derive great happiness and fulfillment through serving ourselves, each other, our families, and friends what we know to be true . . . that food mixed with love is powerful medicine for body and soul and should be served up with gratitude and joy!

Not Only for Diabetics

We believe that eating healthy should be enjoyable and inspiring. This practice should also be the experience for the diabetic community. Many of the cookbooks available for the diabetic community are not paying attention to improving overall well-being. They tend to be overly focused on sugar substitutions, rather than on improving vitality, energy, enjoyment, health and wellness. Most are full of synthetic and artificial ingredients, fake sugars, and a non-whole and healthy foods approach. We wanted to change the game! These recipes are perfect for diabetics, great for overall well-being, and will be enjoyed by both diabetics and non-diabetics alike. We encourage and challenge you to not even bother sharing that the recipes came from a cookbook designed for diabetics. Trust us, what they do not know will only make them happier and healthier at mealtime!

The recipes are designed to not only support healthy biomarkers and physiologic response to diabetes—they are also rich in health-affirming and disease-fighting nutrients, antioxidants, and other natural nutrient power houses. They are naturally high in fiber and other anti-inflammatory compounds that have shown to have a positive health effect in diabetics and in the prevention of diabetes. You have the power and the roadmap to chart a brand-new course, one that is all about greater self-awareness, personal empowerment, and inspired vitality.

A Way of Life

Please consider the recipes in this cookbook as a way of life. Diet comes from the Greek word, *diaita*, which means "way of life." Eating well, moving daily, expressing a positive outlook and attitude are also part of a wellness lifestyle. We believe that carbohydrates, protein, and fat are "secondary foods." For true nourishment and a high level of health, well being, and life satisfaction, they follow the "primary foods" of family, friendships, service, purpose, and love. When you have these two "food groups" in order and in healthy abundance, you will thrive in your life. The goal of a healthy diet is simple: enjoyment, satisfaction, and fulfillment. Consider how you wish to lead life . . . balanced, energetic, creative, and meaningful. Good, healthy, and whole foods have the power to deliver that experience every day of your life.

We have great work in front of us. Type 2 diabetes is an epidemic in the United States. This is generally a disease of poor diet and lifestyle choices. This cookbook is not a stand-alone support or one-stop solution. To be successful with managing or even curing type 2 diabetes, you need to embark on a complete lifestyle mission—one that incorporates and integrates daily exercise, rejuvenating sleep, committed stress management and life balance practices, along with healthy, vibrant relationships that nurture both your heart and soul. You have the tools; you have the ability and the opportunity.

Your Time to Shine

All worthy goals are successfully reached by having a vision, a vision that is bigger than you. We have counseled and treated thousands of individuals, and we know that the ones who have the greatest success with truly changing their health and their lives are the ones who connect their desire to change to being "better" and more alive for the ones they love. A healthier blood sugar number is temporarily exciting and empowering. But, when you connect the success of reaching your goals to the ones that you love (the way you want to be there for the things that matter most) now you have the inspiration to make healthy habits and change real . . . and that will last a long and healthy lifetime. This is your life on purpose. This is your call to loving action. And this is your time to shine your healthiest and brightest light!

It is our honor and privilege to share and serve. We wish you every blessing on your journey towards greater health, happiness, and optimum wellness.

—Drs. James and Debra Rouse

Understanding Diabetes

1 Diabetes means that your blood glucose (sugar) is too high. Your blood always has some glucose in it because the body uses glucose for energy; it's the fuel that keeps you going. But too much glucose in the blood is not good for your health.

The key element in diabetes is insulin, a hormone that allows glucose (sugar) to be converted into energy. The onset of diabetes indicates that the body is experiencing a shortage of insulin and/or decreased ability to use it.

Type 1 diabetes, which is caused by the inability of the pancreas to produce insulin, usually manifests early in children and young adults under age thirty. It accounts for about 5% of cases. Type 2 diabetes, in which the body fails to respond appropriately to the presence of insulin and to properly absorb glucose from the blood, accounts for 95% of incidences, generally occurring after age forty.

2 Your body changes most of the food you eat into glucose. Your blood takes the glucose to the cells throughout your body. The glucose needs insulin to get into the body's cells. Insulin is a hormone made in the pancreas, an organ near the stomach. The pancreas releases insulin into the blood. Insulin helps the glucose from food get into body cells. If your body does not make enough insulin or the insulin does not work right, the glucose can't get into the cells, so it stays in the blood. This makes your blood glucose level high, which may lead to diabetes.

3 Complementary treatment of type 2 diabetes begins with simple nutrition and exercise recommendations. In women, diabetes can cause problems during pregnancy and increase the risk of complications and/or birth defects.

4 Family history, ethnicity, and obesity all play a major role in the possible development of type 2 diabetes. Following a diet based on low-glycemic carbohydrates (carbs), adequate protein, and good fats is the first step.

- Examples of "good" (low-glycemic) carbs include legumes and beans, whole wheat, barley, brown rice, quinoa, apples, apricots, grapefruit, cherries, plums, pears, and berries.
- Examples of "bad" (high-glycemic) carbs include (but are not limited to) donuts, white rice and white flour products, cookies, cake, and dried dates.
- Healthy proteins include lean chicken and turkey, wild salmon, grass-fed beef and buffalo, tofu and tempeh, and eggs.
- Healthy fats come from olive oil, flax seed oil, hemp seed oil, canola oil, grapeseed oil, avocados, and coconuts.

5   Fruit contains naturally occurring sugars, which if eaten in excessive amounts, would not be the best choice for individuals with diabetes. However, most fruit also contains a high amount of vitamins, minerals, fiber, and phytonutrients that support overall health and wellness. Where we need to be cautious is in the use of fruit juice, which contains little to no fiber and a much higher concentration of sugar.

A high-fiber diet is important to help improve blood sugar and the insulin response. Low-fiber diets have been associated with an increased risk for diabetes. Foods to include are whole grains, nuts, seeds, and dark green leafy vegetables.

6   Physical activity and aerobic exercise support healthy weight management and may help control blood glucose. Exercise helps with circulation and helps prevent some of the complications of diabetes, including peripheral vascular disease and heart disease.

7   In general, a normal fasting adult blood glucose level is between 70 and 99 milligrams/deciliter (mg/dL). A random sample may range up to 125 mg/dL and blood glucose measured two hours after eating may range up to 145mg/dL. A higher than average result may signal possible diabetes. For example, a fasting blood glucose level about 125 mg/dL (or a random sample above 200 mg/dL) on at least two different days meets the criteria for diagnosing diabetes. Still, there are other medical conditions that can cause blood glucose levels to be elevated including: stroke, major stress, and some medications.

8   When diagnosed early and treated aggressively with lifestyle measures, such as nutrition and exercise and possibly medications, type 2 diabetes can be reversible.

This book is not intended to treat or diagnose type 1 or type 2 diabetes. We emphatically urge you to work along with your physician in managing your diabetes. If you have type 1 diabetes, you will need to be managed with insulin and/or possibly additional medications, in addition to maintaining a healthy diet and lifestyle. Conventional medical treatment of type 2 diabetes typically starts with lifestyle and dietary changes, including aerobic and resistance exercise and avoidance of excess carbohydrates, sweets, and starches. If necessary, a glucose-lowering medication may be added.

Beverages & Appetizers

Mock Milkshake

Mock Milkshake

6 ounces almond milk
(unsweetened)

1 cup ice cubes

1 scoop whey protein

1 tablespoon cocoa powder

1 Blend all ingredients until smooth.

PER SERVING

123 Calories	0g Sugar*
1g Fat (trace fat)	2g Dietary Fiber
26g Protein	0mg Cholesterol
4g Carbohydrates	158mg Sodium

*0g Sugar is based on using a vanilla whey protein powder flavored with Stevia.

Chai Tea

Makes 4 servings

4 cups water

1 tablespoon chopped fresh ginger

1 cinnamon stick

4 whole cloves

⅛ teaspoon ground cardamom

4 black tea bags

4 teaspoons honey (optional, for sweet chai)

½ cup 2% milk

1 Combine water, fresh ginger, and ground spices; bring to a low boil. Reduce heat, and simmer about 10 minutes.

2 Turn off heat, and add tea bags to the herbal water. Allow to steep about 4 minutes. Stir in honey, if desired.

3 Add milk to the tea mixture, and warm to desired drinking temperature. Strain before serving.

PER SERVING (1 cup)

73 Calories	7g Sugar
2g Fat (1g sat)	4g Dietary Fiber
2g Protein	2mg Cholesterol
15g Carbohydrates	42mg Sodium

Super Berry Green Smoothie

Makes 1 serving

This smoothie will be a lovely green color! Admittedly, this is a go-to recipe when we're pressed for time or need a quick dose of high-impact nutrition. Don't be afraid of the greens; you won't taste them.

6 ounces 2% milk of choice (cow's, almond, soy, rice, oat)

½ cup chopped frozen organic strawberries

1 cup kale, spinach, chard, or collards

1 scoop vanilla protein powder (we prefer whey or brown rice protein)

1 Add all of the ingredients to a blender fitted tightly with lid. Blend until desired creamy consistency is achieved.

PER SERVING

243 Calories	3.5g Sugar
1g Fat (trace sat)	4g Dietary Fiber
28g Protein	0mg Cholesterol
35g Carbohydrates	180mg Sodium

Funky Monkey Smoothie

Makes 1 serving

6 ounces almond milk (for homemade Almond Milk, see page 15)

1 teaspoon almond butter

½ medium banana (frozen will make a thicker smoothie)

1 scoop whey protein

1 tablespoon plain nonfat Greek-style yogurt

1 teaspoon cocoa powder (optional)

1 Add all ingredients to a blender, and process until smooth and creamy.

PER SERVING

209 Calories	8g Sugar
4g Fat (1g sat)	2g Dietary Fiber
28g Protein	1mg Cholesterol
17g Carbohydrates	160mg Sodium

Almond "Milk"

Makes about 6 servings

You'll need a good blender for this recipe. Enjoy in smoothies, granola, oatmeal, recipes that call for milk, or sip alone. We personally feel it doesn't need anything else, but some folks like to add a bit of vanilla and honey or maple syrup for sweetness.

1½ cups raw almonds

Pure water for soaking

6 cups water for blending

Cheesecloth or nutmilk bag

A nutmilk bag makes this much easier and more enjoyable. You can find them online at Pure Joy Planet, but many local grocers carry them, so check with yours.

1 Soak almonds in pure water overnight. Drain and rinse well with pure, cold water.

2 Add the almonds to your blender plus 6 cups of pure, filtered water. Make sure the lid for your blender is on tight because the water/milk will likely want to burst out the top. Blend on high until nuts are completely pulverized.

3 Make sure your hands are very clean before you start this process. Pour the blended mixture slowly through cheesecloth or a nutmilk bag into a large (8-cup) mason jar or other large container. We usually make this in a few pours rather than trying to get it all done at once. Gently squeeze the milk out until you are left with a ball of almond pulp. Refrigerate and save the pulp to make crackers (if you aren't going to use it up within a few days, then we recommend freezing it in an airtight container or freezer bag).

4 Shake or stir the milk before using.

PER SERVING (1 cup)

35 Calories	0g Sugar
2.5g Fat (0 sat)	0g Dietary Fiber
1g Protein	0mg Cholesterol
2g Carbohydrates	15mg Sodium

NOTE: These nutritional amounts may vary depending on precise measurements of almonds, blending time, and concentration of milk.

Peach Sangria Spritzer

Makes 1½ quarts (6 servings)

This obviously isn't an everyday splurge, but it's fun for an occasional celebration.

3 cups red wine

⅓ cup freshly squeezed orange juice

⅓ cup peach nectar

2 peaches, quartered and sliced

2 cups club soda

Fresh slices of orange (optional)

1 In a large pitcher, stir together wine, orange juice, and peach nectar. Refrigerate 2–3 hours to allow flavors to mingle.

2 About 1 hour before serving, add peaches.

3 Add club soda just before serving. Pour into glasses filled with ice. Garnish with orange slices, if desired.

PER SERVING (1 cup)

109 Calories	7.3g Sugar
trace Fat	1g Dietary Fiber
1g Protein	0mg Cholesterol
8g Carbohydrates	76mg Sodium

Veggie Chips

Makes about 6 servings

1 pound kale

2 tablespoons olive oil, divided

¼ teaspoon salt, divided

¼ teaspoon pepper, divided

1 medium yam

1 medium zucchini

If you have a food dehydrator, you can place the veggie slices on drying racks and set temperature to 115°. Dry for 4–8 hours, removing kale once it has dried.

1 Preheat an oven to 300°. Line 2 large non-insulated baking sheets with parchment paper.

2 Tear the kale leaves from the thick stems (or slice off carefully with a knife). Wash well, spin dry with a salad spinner, and allow to thoroughly dry on a clean kitchen towel. Toss kale with a tablespoon of olive oil; use clean hands to massage the oil into the leaves. Season lightly with ⅛ teaspoon each of salt and pepper. Distribute kale evenly on one of the prepared baking sheets.

3 Slice the yam and zucchini with a mandolin slicer to achieve even, thin slices, about ⅛ inch thick. Drizzle remaining 1 tablespoon olive oil on top of vegetables, and toss to coat. Sprinkle with ⅛ teaspoon each of salt and pepper, and toss again. Distribute vegetables evenly on second baking sheet.

4 Bake until the edges are slightly brown but not burnt, about 10 minutes for the kale, and up to 20 minutes for the other vegetables.

5 When all of the veggies are equally crisp, toss together and serve. Season with additional herbs and spices as desired.

PER SERVING (about 1 cup chips)

112 Calories	<1g Sugar
5g Fat (1g sat)	3g Dietary Fiber
3g Protein	0mg Cholesterol
16g Carbohydrates	125mg Sodium

Almond Flax Crackers

Almond Flax Crackers

Makes about 36 crackers

1 cup almond pulp (or almond meal with 1 tablespoon water added)

2 tablespoons ground flax

1 tablespoon olive or canola oil

1 tablespoon honey or agave nectar

½ teaspoon sea salt

⅛ teaspoon pepper

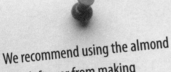

We recommend using the almond pulp left over from making Almond "Milk" (page 15).

1 Preheat oven to 175°.

2 Combine all ingredients in a large bowl. Stir together until very well mixed.

3 Roll dough into a ball. Flatten between 2 pieces of wax paper or plastic wrap; roll into a flat rectangle, about ⅛ inch thick.

4 Remove top piece of wax paper or plastic. Flip the bottom piece onto a large baking sheet lined with parchment paper. Gently slice dough into small squares (about 1½ inches) with a knife or pizza slicer.

5 Bake for about 70 minutes or until tops of crackers feel dry. Remove from oven, and allow to cool completely before sampling or serving.

NOTE: Alternatively, you can use a food dehydrator instead of baking: flip the rolled mixture onto a dehydrator grid, set temperature to 115°, and dehydrate for about 12 hours.

PER SERVING (2 crackers)

50 Calories	2g Sugar
2g Fat (trace sat)	trace Dietary Fiber
3g Protein	0mg Cholesterol
4g Carbohydrates	53mg Sodium

Skinny Spinach Artichoke Dip

Makes 1½ cups (6 servings)

This is delicious enough to eat with a spoon. Feel free to experiment with different greens, like kale or chard.

5 ounces baby spinach

9 ounces artichoke hearts (liquid drained)

1 small shallot, chopped

2 tablespoons mascarpone cheese

¼ cup low-fat ricotta cheese

¼ teaspoon salt

⅛ teaspoon white pepper

1 Add spinach to bowl of food processor, and pulse to chop.

2 Add artichoke hearts and shallot, and pulse again until vegetables are minced.

3 Add both cheeses, salt, and pepper, and purée until smooth.

4 Cover, and refrigerate at least 30 minutes before serving.

PER SERVING (¼ cup)

60 Calories	1.5g Sugar
3g Fat (2g sat)	3g Dietary Fiber
4g Protein	11mg Cholesterol
6g Carbohydrates	199mg Sodium

Dr. James Rouse

White Bean and Roasted Red Pepper Dip or Spread

Makes 1¼ cups (5 servings)

1 cup cannellini beans, soaked and cooked (or use canned)

1 clove garlic, minced

2 tablespoons chopped shallots

1½ medium red bell peppers, roasted

1 tablespoon lemon juice

1 tablespoon olive oil

½ teaspoon salt

¼ teaspoon pepper

1 In a food processor or blender, purée all ingredients, stopping and scraping down the sides as necessary.

2 Transfer purée to a glass or ceramic bowl. Refrigerate for at least 1 hour before serving.

3 Serve at room temperature with raw vegetables and/or whole-grain crackers.

PER SERVING (¼ cup)

94 Calories	1.5g Sugar
3g Fat (trace sat)	3g Dietary Fiber
4g Protein	0mg Cholesterol
14g Carbohydrates	217mg Sodium

Edamame-Feta Spread

Makes 1⅓ cups (4 servings)

2 cups shelled edamame (if frozen, thaw first)

2 cloves garlic, minced

½ cup crumbled feta cheese

2½ tablespoons lemon juice

2 tablespoons extra virgin olive oil

¼ teaspoon sea salt

¼ teaspoon black pepper

1 Mix and mash all ingredients together by hand or with a blender or food processor.

2 Serve with crackers, chips, rice cakes, or veggies.

PER SERVING (⅓ cup)

129 Calories	1.2g Sugar
8g Fat (2g sat)	3g Dietary Fiber
8g Protein	8mg Cholesterol
7g Carbohydrates	167mg Sodium

Hummus

Makes 2 cups (8 servings)

1 (15-ounce) can chickpeas, cooked

2 tablespoons sesame tahini

1 clove garlic, minced

1 tablespoon olive oil

¼ teaspoon ground cumin

¼ teaspoon salt

2 tablespoons fresh lemon juice

Water, as needed to thin

1 teaspoon chopped fresh parsley

1 Combine the chickpeas, tahini, garlic, olive oil, cumin, salt, and lemon juice in a food processor; process until smooth. Add water to thin, as necessary.

2 Place in a serving bowl, and garnish with fresh parsley.

3 Spread on crackers, or use as a dip for raw vegetables.

PER SERVING (¼ cup)

233 Calories	1g Sugar
7g Fat (1g sat)	10g Dietary Fiber
11g Protein	0mg Cholesterol
34g Carbohydrates	84mg Sodium

Hummus is amazingly versatile. Experiment with different add-ins like roasted red bell pepper, sun-dried tomatoes, olives, artichoke hearts, red onion, black beans, or spinach.

Babaganoush

Eggplant is a good source of fiber, and vitamins and minerals, including vitamins K, C, B6, folate, and niacin, as well as magnesium and potassium.

1 medium eggplant, sliced in half

1 teaspoon olive oil

¼ cup tahini (sesame seed paste or "butter")

1 tablespoon lemon juice

1 clove garlic

⅛ teaspoon black pepper

⅛ teaspoon salt

Dash of ground cumin

2 tablespoons sesame seeds

2 tablespoons finely chopped fresh parsley (more, for garnish, if desired)

1 Preheat oven to 425°.

2 Brush eggplant with olive oil on fleshy side. Roast eggplant for 30 minutes or until flesh is smoky and tender.

3 Scoop out the flesh, and discard the skin. Drain any excess liquid from the eggplant, and place in a food processor fitted with the S blade.

4 Add tahini, lemon juice, and garlic. Pulse to combine.

5 Stir in remaining ingredients; spoon into serving bowl. Garnish with parsley sprig. Serve warm or chilled.

PER SERVING (3 tablespoons)

125 Calories	<1g Sugar
10g Fat (1g sat)	4g Dietary Fiber
4g Protein	0mg Cholesterol
9g Carbohydrates	63mg Sodium

BEVERAGES & APPETIZERS

Watermelon Tomato Towers

Watermelon Tomato Towers

Makes 4 servings

Watermelon contains wonderful nutrients like vitamins A and C, and potassium.

1¼ cups sliced seedless watermelon (1 to 2 wedges)

3 medium yellow tomatoes

1 teaspoon olive oil

1 teaspoon balsamic vinegar

1 ounce crumbled goat cheese

1 tablespoon finely chopped fresh basil

1 Slice the watermelon into thin slices, no thicker than ¼ inch. Remove the rind, and cut square portions of watermelon so that it will stand out when you alternate with slices of tomato.

2 Slice the tomatoes, also no thicker than ¼-inch slices.

3 Stack, alternating 3 squares of watermelon with 3 slices of ripe tomato.

4 Drizzle each stack with olive oil and balsamic vinegar. Sprinkle crumbled goat cheese and fresh basil on and around the stacks.

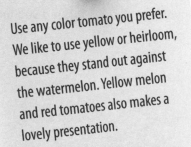

Use any color tomato you prefer. We like to use yellow or heirloom, because they stand out against the watermelon. Yellow melon and red tomatoes also makes a lovely presentation.

PER SERVING (1 tower)

79 Calories	6g Sugar
4g Fat (2g sat)	1g Dietary Fiber
4g Protein	7mg Cholesterol
8g Carbohydrates	62mg Sodium

Curried Deviled Eggs

6 hard-boiled eggs

2 tablespoons mayonnaise

2 tablespoons plain Greek-style yogurt

½ teaspoon curry powder

⅛ teaspoon each: salt and pepper (or to taste)

6 fresh basil leaves, chopped

We often leave out the mayonnaise altogether and simply use plain Greek-style yogurt.

1 Slice the eggs in half lengthwise. Separate the yolks from the whites, and reserve the whites separately.

2 Mash the egg yolks with the mayonnaise, yogurt, and curry powder. Blend with an electric mixer for smoothest results. Stir or blend in salt and pepper to taste.

3 Pipe or spoon the yolk mixture into the cavities of the egg whites. Garnish with chopped fresh basil.

PER SERVING (2 halves)

111 Calories	<1g Sugar
9g Fat (2g sat)	trace Dietary Fiber
7g Protein	214mg Cholesterol
1g Carbohydrates	129mg Sodium

Chorizo Stuffed Mini Peppers

Makes 6 servings

12 medium mini bell peppers

3 ounces goat cheese

3 ounces chorizo, cooked

1 Preheat oven to 375°. Line a large baking sheet with parchment.

2 Cut the tops off of the peppers, and remove the seeds.

3 Combine goat cheese and cooked chorizo in small bowl. Carefully spoon the mixture into the peppers.

4 Bake until heated through, about 20 minutes. Cool before serving.

PER SERVING (2 peppers)

143 Calories	0 Sugar
10g Fat (6g sat)	trace Dietary Fiber
8g Protein	27mg Cholesterol
1g Carbohydrates	224mg Sodium

Sweet Potato Goat Cheese Stacks

Sweet Potato Goat Cheese Stacks

Makes about 4 servings

2 medium sweet potatoes

1 teaspoon olive oil

4 ounces goat cheese

Salt and pepper to taste

Cinnamon (optional)

1 Preheat oven to 400°.

2 Slice sweet potatoes across their width into ¼-inch round discs. Brush with a little olive oil; place in a single layer on 2 baking sheets.

3 Roast sweet potatoes in the oven 20–25 minutes or until softened and starting to brown.

4 Remove from oven, and while warm, place 1 slice (about ½ ounce or 1 tablespoon) goat cheese on top of 1 slice of sweet potato, then top with another slice of sweet potato. Repeat until all slices are used.

5 Season to taste with salt and pepper. Also delicious with a sprinkle of cinnamon on top.

6 Serve over salad or sautéed greens.

PER SERVING (2 stacks)

206 Calories	2.5g Sugar
11g Fat (7g sat)	2g Dietary Fiber
10g Protein	30mg Cholesterol
16g Carbohydrates	107mg Sodium

Salmon Cucumber Bites

Makes about 8 servings

2 large English cucumbers, washed
   and sliced

½ cup cottage cheese

2 tablespoons mascarpone cheese

2 tablespoons Greek-style yogurt

3 ounces smoked chinook salmon

1 small shallot, chopped

1 tablespoon lemon juice

1 teaspoon chopped dill

1 dash each: salt and pepper

1 Slice cucumber into ½- to ¾-inch rounds (discard or compost the ends). Use a melon ball scooper to make a small hollow cup in the top, discarding seeds.

2 Combine the cottage cheese, mascarpone, and yogurt in a blender or food processor, and process until smooth.

3 Add smoked salmon pieces, chopped shallot, lemon juice, dill, salt, and pepper, and process again until smooth.

4 Spoon or pipe about 1 tablespoon salmon mixture into the top of the cucumbers. Refrigerate until ready to serve.

PER SERVING (3 "bites")

56 Calories	<1g Sugar
3g Fat (1g sat)	1g Dietary Fiber
6g Protein	9mg Cholesterol
3g Carbohydrates	168mg Sodium

Bread & Baked Goods

Zucchini Chocolate Chip Bread

Zucchini Chocolate Chip Bread

Makes 8 servings

2 eggs

¼ cup safflower oil

½ cup granulated sugar

1 teaspoon vanilla extract

1½ cups whole-wheat pastry flour

1 teaspoon ground cinnamon

¼ teaspoon salt

1 teaspoon baking soda

1 teaspoon baking powder

1 cup finely grated zucchini, drained

¼ cup dark chocolate or semisweet mini chips (optional)

1 Preheat oven to 350°. Prepare 8-inch loaf pan by coating it with cooking oil spray.

2 In a medium bowl, beat eggs with an electric beater. Add oil, sugar, and vanilla, and beat again until smooth and custardy.

3 In another bowl, combine flour thoroughly with cinnamon, salt, baking soda, and baking powder, and mix together with a wooden spoon. Stir in wet ingredients.

4 Add zucchini and chocolate chips, and stir until well mixed.

5 Spoon batter into prepared loaf pan.

6 Bake on center rack in oven for about 50 minutes or until wooden skewer or toothpick comes out clean.

To dramatically lower the sugar content in this recipe, omit the chocolate chips, and reduce the sugar to ¼ cup. That will bring the sugar per serving total to about 6g.

PER SERVING

227 Calories	16g Sugar
11g Fat (2g sat)	3g Dietary Fiber
5g Protein	53mg Cholesterol
36g Carbohydrates	370mg Sodium

Carrot Breakfast Bread

Makes 10 servings

This is a delicious, not-too-sweet bread that we like to enjoy as part of a healthy breakfast. It is especially good with a little bit of almond butter spread on top.

1 cup whole-wheat pastry flour

1 cup whole-wheat flour

2 tablespoons ground flax

⅓ cup rolled oats

2 teaspoons baking powder

½ teaspoon baking soda

½ teaspoon ground cinnamon

¼ teaspoon nutmeg

¼ teaspoon ground ginger

¼ cup chopped walnuts

3 eggs

¼ cup oil

¼ cup brown sugar

½ cup unsweetened applesauce

1 cup grated carrots

1 Preheat oven to 325°. Prepare a 5x9-inch bread loaf pan by coating with cooking oil spray.

2 Whisk together flours, ground flax, oats, baking powder, baking soda, spices, and nuts in large bowl.

3 In a separate bowl, beat eggs until foamy. Stir in oil, brown sugar, applesauce, and grated carrots.

4 Add liquid ingredients to dry ingredients. Stir until just mixed.

5 Pour into greased loaf pan. Bake for 50–60 minutes, using toothpick to test for doneness.

6 Cool on a wire rack for at least 15 minutes before removing from pan.

PER SERVING

282 Calories	2.3g Sugar
12g Fat (2g sat)	6g Dietary Fiber
8g Protein	80mg Cholesterol
34g Carbohydrates	237mg Sodium

Applesauce Oat Nut Bread

Makes about 10 servings

1 cup applesauce

3 egg whites

¼ cup safflower oil

¼ cup 2% milk

½ cup sugar

1 cup rolled oats

1½ cups whole-wheat pastry flour

1 teaspoon baking powder

1 teaspoon baking soda

¼ teaspoon salt

1 teaspoon ground cinnamon

¼ teaspoon ground nutmeg

TOPPING:

1 tablespoon unsalted butter

½ cup rolled oats

2 tablespoons brown sugar

¼ teaspoon cinnamon

¼ cup chopped walnuts

1 Preheat oven to 350°. Prepare 5x9-inch bread pan by coating with cooking spray.

2 In a large mixing bowl, whisk together applesauce, egg whites, oil, milk, and sugar.

3 In a separate bowl, mix together oats, flour, baking powder, baking soda, salt, cinnamon, and nutmeg.

4 Stir dry ingredients into wet until just mixed. Pour batter into prepared baking pan.

5 For Topping, melt butter on the stovetop or in a glass bowl in the microwave. Stir in ½ cup oats, brown sugar, cinnamon, and chopped walnuts. Spoon Topping on top of batter.

6 Bake for about 55 minutes to an hour.

PER SERVING

289 Calories	16g Sugar
12g Fat (2g sat)	5g Dietary Fiber
7g Protein	4mg Cholesterol
40g Carbohydrates	249mg Sodium

Cherry Oat Muffins

Cherry Oat Muffins

Makes 12 muffins

The vanilla flavor blends itself nicely here with the tart cherries. Tart cherries have been touted as a "super fruit" due to their high antioxidant content. Like any dried fruit though, you want to limit your intake, because as fruit dries, the sugars concentrate, making dried fruits much higher in sugar content than their fresh counterparts. Fresh tart cherries have a potential effect of reducing insulin and fasting glucose levels.

1 cup old-fashioned or quick-cooking oats, uncooked

1 cup Gluten-Free Flour Mixture (page 44)

½ cup firmly packed brown sugar

1½ teaspoons baking powder

¼ teaspoon ground nutmeg

1 egg, slightly beaten

½ cup 2% milk

¼ cup plain Greek-style yogurt

¼ cup safflower oil

1 teaspoon vanilla extract

½ cup unsweetened dried cherries, coarsely chopped

1 Preheat oven top 400°.

2 Whisk together egg, milk, yogurt, oil, and vanilla extract in a separate bowl.

3 Pour liquid mixture into oats mixture; stir just to moisten ingredients. Stir in cherries.

4 Spray muffin pan with nonstick cooking oil spray or line with baking cups. Fill muffin cups about three-quarters full.

5 Bake in a preheated 400° oven 15 minutes.

6 Bake for about 15 minutes, allowing to cool on rack for 5 minutes before removing muffins from pan.

We made these gluten free, but you can absolutely substitute whole-wheat pastry flour or all-purpose flour for the Gluten-Free Flour Mixture.

PER MUFFIN

127 Calories	10.5g Sugar
6g Fat (1g sat)	1g Dietary Fiber
3g Protein	19mg Cholesterol
17g Carbohydrates	79mg Sodium

Island Muffins

Makes about 6 muffins

1⅓ cups Gluten-Free Flour Mixture, page 44 (or whole-wheat pastry flour)

1 teaspoon baking powder

⅓ cup sugar

½ teaspoon cinnamon

⅓ cup lite coconut milk

1 medium egg

1 tablespoon grapeseed oil

1 teaspoon vanilla extract

⅓ cup diced fresh mango

⅓ cup chopped pecans

CRUMBLE TOPPING: (Optional)

2 tablespoons rolled oats

2 tablespoons chopped pecans

1 tablespoon brown sugar

2 tablespoons unsweetened shredded coconut

1 tablespoon coconut oil

1. Preheat oven to 350°. Prepare a 6-cup muffin tin with parchment paper muffin cups.

2. Combine, and stir together dry ingredients in a medium mixing bowl.

3. In a separate bowl, whisk coconut milk, egg, oil, and vanilla extract.

4. Stir wet ingredients into dry until just incorporated. Add mango and pecans, and gently stir until the fruit and nuts are well incorporated.

5. Fill lined muffin cups about three-quarters full. You can bake these for 18 minutes as-is, or for slightly more tropical decadence, add the Crumble Topping.

6. For Crumble Topping, add rolled oats, pecans, brown sugar, shredded coconut, and coconut oil to the bowl of a food processor fitted with S blade. Pulse together until crumbly.

7. Spoon 1 heaping teaspoon of this mixture onto the muffin batter.

8. Bake about 18 minutes or until toothpick comes out clean. Cool at least 5 minutes on a wire rack before removing from pan.

PER MUFFIN (without topping)

218 Calories	14g Sugar
15g Fat (7g sat)	2g Dietary Fiber
2g Protein	35mg Cholesterol
18g Carbohydrates	99mg Sodium

Strawberry Flax Muffins

Makes 12 muffins

1½ cups whole-wheat pastry flour

¼ cup ground flax

¼ cup oat bran

2 teaspoons baking powder

¼ teaspoon salt

1 egg, beaten

¼ cup grapeseed or canola oil

½ cup milk

½ teaspoon vanilla

½ cup natural cane sugar (or brown sugar)

1 cup diced strawberries

1 Preheat oven to 350°. Prepare a 12-cup muffin pan with nonstick cooking oil spray or paper liners.

2 In a large bowl, whisk together flour, ground flax, oat bran, baking powder, and salt until well mixed.

3 In a medium bowl, beat together egg, oil, milk, and vanilla. Beat in sugar.

4 Add wet ingredients to dry ingredients, and gently stir together until just combined.

5 Stir in diced strawberries.

6 Scoop batter into prepared muffin pan, about two-thirds full.

7 Bake muffins for 18–20 minutes, until edges just start to brown and muffins are cooked through (when a toothpick inserted into the middle of the muffin comes out clean).

8 Cool on a wire rack for at least 10 minutes before trying to remove from pan.

PER MUFFIN

166 Calories	9.2g Sugar
6g Fat (1g sat)	4g Dietary Fiber
3g Protein	19mg Cholesterol
22g Carbohydrates	140mg Sodium

Pumpkin Spice Muffins

Makes 16 muffins

2½ cups whole-wheat pastry flour

1 teaspoon baking soda

½ teaspoon baking powder

½ teaspoon nutmeg

½ teaspoon cinnamon

¼ teaspoon ground ginger

4 tablespoons softened butter

½ cup granulated sugar

2 tablespoons maple syrup

¼ cup Greek-style yogurt

1 teaspoon vanilla extract

½ teaspoon maple extract

2 eggs

15 ounces pumpkin purée (1¾ cups)

1 Preheat oven to 350°. Line 16 standard muffin tins with baking cups.

2 Sift the flour, baking soda, baking powder, and spices together twice. Set aside.

3 Beat butter, sugar, maple syrup, yogurt, vanilla and maple extracts, and eggs together until fluffy. Stir in the pumpkin.

4 Fold in the dry ingredients, being careful not to overmix.

5 Scoop into lined muffin pans.

6 Bake at 350° until brown and firm, approximately 22 minutes. Muffins should be moist and steamy inside.

PER MUFFIN

147 Calories	3g Dietary Fiber
4g Fat (2g sat)	35mg Cholesterol
3g Protein	136mg Sodium
25g Carbohydrates	
8.5g Sugar	

Apple Streusel Coffee Cake

Makes 12 servings

3 eggs

1 cup unsweetened applesauce

½ cup unsalted butter, melted

½ cup Greek-style yogurt

1 teaspoon vanilla extract

1 teaspoon ground cinnamon

¼ teaspoon grated nutmeg

¾ cup grated apple

2 cups whole-wheat pastry flour

2 teaspoons ground flax

1 teaspoon baking powder

1 teaspoon baking soda

STREUSEL:

¼ cup whole-wheat flour

¼ cup brown sugar

½ teaspoon cinnamon

1 tablespoon unsalted butter, melted

1 Preheat oven to 350°. Prepare 8x13-inch cake pan by coating with cooking spray.

2 Beat eggs with an electric beater, or stand-up mixer fitted with a whisk, for about a minute until well beaten.

3 Add applesauce, melted butter, yogurt, vanilla extract, cinnamon, and nutmeg. Beat on medium for another few minutes until well mixed. Stir in grated apple.

4 In separate bowl, whisk together flour, ground flax, baking powder, and baking soda. Add dry ingredients to wet, and stir or blend briefly to combine. Scrape down sides of bowl, if necessary.

5 Add batter to prepared cake pan.

6 Combine Streusel ingredients in a small bowl. Sprinkle a light coating of Streusel over the top of the cake batter.

7 Bake on middle rack for 50 minutes or until toothpick inserted comes out clean.

PER SERVING

215 Calories	8g Sugar
11g Fat (6g sat)	4g Dietary Fiber
5g Protein	77mg Cholesterol
25g Carbohydrates	172mg Sodium

Lemon-Almond-Oat Scones

Lemon-Almond-Oat Scones

Makes 12 Scones

1¼ cups whole-wheat pastry flour (plus a little extra for kneading)

½ cup rolled oats

3 tablespoons sugar

2 teaspoons baking powder

½ teaspoon sea salt

2 teaspoons grated lemon peel

⅓ cup cold butter, cut into small pieces

2 tablespoons lemon juice

1 egg, beaten

½ cup sliced or slivered almonds

4 tablespoons milk

1 egg, beaten

1 Preheat oven to 400°.

2 In the bowl of a food processor fitted with S blade, combine wheat flour, oats, sugar, baking powder, sea salt, and lemon peel. Pulse to combine.

3 Add butter piece by piece to the flour mixture, and pulse a few times until mixture resembles fine crumbs.

4 Add the lemon juice and 1 egg, and pulse again 2–3 times. Add the almonds and milk, and pulse a few more times until the batter just starts to leave the sides of the bowl.

5 Turn dough onto lightly floured surface; gently roll in flour to coat. Knead lightly 10 times.

6 Roll or pat to ½-inch thickness. Cut with floured 2-inch round cutter, or cut into triangles with sharp knife.

7 Place on ungreased cookie sheet. Brush remaining egg over dough.

8 Bake for 18–20 minutes until lightly golden.

PER SERVING (1 scone)

216 Calories	3.5g Sugar
12g Fat (5g sat)	4g Dietary Fiber
6g Protein	60mg Cholesterol
23g Carbohydrates	272mg Sodium

Gluten-Free Flour Mixture

Makes 6 cups

This is a pretty flexible recipe. Most of the flours are available at natural food stores. If not, you can definitely find them online. If you don't have amaranth flour, you can substitute more rice flour or gluten-free oat flour. You can also add ground flax to boost the fiber content.

Since two of our family members are gluten intolerant, we almost always use this mixture for our baked goods, pancakes, and waffles. For the recipes in this cookbook, feel free to substitute equal amounts of this flour mixture in place of whole-wheat pastry flour or all-purpose flour and vice versa. If you don't have a problem with gluten, then by all means feel free to substitute whole-wheat pastry flour for the gluten-free mixture.

3 cups brown rice flour

1 cup white rice flour

1 cup amaranth flour

½ cup almond meal

¼ cup potato starch

¼ cup tapioca flour

1 tablespoon xanthan gum

1 Whisk all the ingredients together until well combined and evenly distributed.

2 Store in airtight container.

PER SERVING (¼ cup)

147 Calories	0g Sugar
2g Fat (1g sat)	2g Dietary Fiber
4g Protein	0mg Cholesterol
30g Carbohydrates	2mg Sodium

Pre-packaged gluten-free flour mix can be high glycemic, especially those that contain mostly white rice flour and cornstarch. Many also add sugar, so be sure to read the label.

Breakfast

Quinoa Breakfast Cakes

Quinoa Breakfast Cakes

Makes 6 servings

1 cup quinoa

2 cups low-sodium vegetable broth

4 large eggs, beaten

1 cup oats

1 small yellow onion, finely chopped

¼ cup freshly grated manchego or Asiago cheese

½ cup finely chopped baby spinach (or other greens)

¼ cup finely shredded carrot

1 pinch garlic powder

¼ teaspoon each: salt and pepper

Chipotle Hollandaise Sauce, page 119 (optional)

PER SERVING (2 cakes)

298 Calories	1g Sugar
8g Fat (2g sat)	6g Dietary Fiber
17g Protein	146mg Cholesterol
39g Carbohydrates	345mg Sodium

1 Combine well-rinsed, uncooked quinoa with vegetable broth. Bring to a boil, cover, reduce heat to low, and simmer for 15–20 minutes, until the quinoa is tender and liquid has been absorbed.

2 Beat the eggs in a medium mixing bowl. Stir in 1 cup cooked quinoa (save the rest for another recipe) and oats. Add the onion, cheese, spinach, carrot, garlic, salt, and pepper. Mix well, and let sit for a few minutes so the oats can absorb some of the moisture. Form the mixture into 10–12 small patties.

3 Heat a large heavy skillet coated with cooking oil spray over medium heat. Add patties to skillet so that they are not too crowded (5–6 should fit). Cook for about 6 minutes.

4 Carefully flip the patties with a spatula, and cook the second sides for 4 minutes (uncovered), or until golden. Check the underside to prevent burning (you may need to reduce heat further, depending on the type of skillet you are using).

5 Remove the patties from the skillet to a plate lined with a paper towel or cloth kitchen towel while you cook the remaining patties. You may also keep them warm in a low-temperature oven.

6 Serve with a side of Chipotle Hollandaise Sauce, if desired.

Breakfast Bars

Makes 14 servings

½ cup honey or agave nectar

½ cup almond butter or peanut butter

2 tablespoons maple syrup

1 tablespoon grapeseed oil

¼ cup dried unsweetened blueberries

¼ cup light brown sugar

¼ teaspoon ground cinnamon

1 teaspoon vanilla or maple extract

2 cups rolled oats

2 cups crispy rice cereal

¼ cup ground flax

¼ teaspoon sea salt

1 Spray a 9x13-inch baking dish with cooking spray, and set aside.

2 In a small saucepan over medium heat, combine honey, almond butter, maple syrup, grapeseed oil, dried blueberries, brown sugar, and cinnamon. Stir, and cook until mixture just begins to bubble, 3–5 minutes. Remove from heat, and stir in vanilla extract.

3 In a large bowl, combine oats, rice cereal, ground flax, and salt.

4 Pour almond butter mixture over oatmeal mixture, and stir gently with a spatula until well combined.

5 Transfer to baking dish, cover with parchment paper, and press firmly into dish. Allow to cool completely (will cool faster in the refrigerator). Cut into squares or bars.

PER SERVING

214 Calories	8g Sugar
7g Fat (1g sat)	3g Dietary Fiber
4g Protein	0mg Cholesterol
32g Carbohydrates	67mg Sodium

Dr. James Rouse

BREAKFAST

Breakfast Tostadas

2 (8-inch) corn tortillas

4 large eggs, beaten

Salt and pepper to taste

¼ cup low-fat, low-sodium refried beans, warmed (stovetop or microwave)

2 tablespoons shredded Monterey Jack cheese

1 cup chopped baby spinach

2 tablespoons chopped cilantro

½ medium avocado, cubed

Salsa

1 Heat tortillas on a medium hot skillet coated with cooking spray, about 1 minute each side. If crispier tortillas are desired, then cook longer. Remove to plate lined with kitchen towel, and keep warm. Recoat the same skillet lightly with cooking oil spray to prepare for eggs.

2 Scramble eggs with salt and pepper to taste. Add to prepared skillet, and cook over medium heat until just cooked through.

3 Spread cooked corn tortillas with warmed refried beans. Sprinkle each with a tablespoon of shredded cheese and ½ cup baby spinach on top of refried beans.

4 Add scrambled eggs on top, and garnish with cilantro and avocado. Top with salsa.

PER SERVING (1 tostada)

421 Calories	1g Sugar
20g Fat (6g sat)	5g Dietary Fiber
20g Protein	430mg Cholesterol
40g Carbohydrates	439mg Sodium

Oatmeal Waffles

Makes 6 servings

1 cup whole-wheat flour

1½ cups rolled oats

1 teaspoon baking powder

½ teaspoon baking soda

½ teaspoon cinnamon

¼ teaspoon salt

2 eggs, slightly beaten

1½ cups low-fat buttermilk

4 tablespoons butter, melted

1 tablespoon sugar

For a fluffier and less chewy waffle, process the oats in a food processor or grain mill until they resemble coarse flour.

1 Preheat a waffle iron, and coat lightly with cooking oil spray.

2 In a large bowl, stir together flour, oats, baking powder, baking soda, cinnamon, and salt.

3 In another bowl, whisk the eggs, milk, butter, and sugar. Add the wet ingredients to the dry, and stir well until combined.

4 Ladle appropriate amount of batter (usually around ⅓ cup) onto preheated and lightly greased waffle iron (amount will vary according to specific waffle maker). Close lid, and cook to desired doneness. Carefully use a fork to remove waffle from the iron.

5 Serve with yogurt, fresh fruit, nut butter, and/or pure maple syrup.

PER SERVING (1 waffle)

271 Calories	3.3g Sugar
12g Fat (6g sat)	5g Dietary Fiber
10g Protein	94mg Cholesterol
34g Carbohydrates	441mg Sodium

Apple Nut Pancakes

Makes 4 servings

1 egg

½ cup 2% milk

½ cup Greek-style yogurt

2 tablespoons unsalted butter, melted

½ teaspoon vanilla extract

1¼ cups whole-wheat pastry flour

1 teaspoon baking powder

1 tablespoon sugar

1 teaspoon cinnamon

¼ teaspoon grated nutmeg

1 small Granny Smith apple, peeled and grated

½ cup chopped walnuts

1 Preheat griddle or skillet to medium high.

2 Whisk the egg with the milk, yogurt, melted butter, and vanilla extract in a large bowl.

3 In another bowl, whisk the flour, baking powder, sugar, cinnamon, and nutmeg.

4 Combine the wet and the dry ingredients, and stir in the grated apples and walnuts.

5 Ladle 2–3 tablespoons of batter onto the griddle or skillet. When they start to bubble, flip the pancakes, and cook them for an additional 2–3 minutes or until lightly browned.

PER SERVING [2 (4-inch) pancakes]

378 Calories	9g Sugar
19g fat (2g sat)	7g Dietary Fiber
13g Protein	57mg Cholesterol
42g Carbohydrates	173mg Sodium

Whole-Grain Blueberry Pancakes

Whole-Grain Blueberry Pancakes

Makes 4 servings

½ cup whole-wheat flour

½ cup brown rice flour

2 tablespoons ground flax

½ teaspoon ground cinnamon

1 teaspoon baking powder

¼ teaspoon baking soda

½ cup low-fat buttermilk

1 medium egg

1 medium egg white

1 teaspoon canola or grapeseed oil

½ cup blueberries (organic or wild preferred, fresh or frozen)

1 Set a nonstick skillet or griddle over medium heat.

2 In a medium bowl, whisk together the wheat flour, rice flour, ground flax, cinnamon, baking powder, and baking soda.

3 In a separate bowl, whisk together the buttermilk, egg, egg white, and oil.

4 Combine the liquid with the dry ingredients, and stir just until moistened.

5 Ladle or spoon about 2 tablespoons of batter onto the prepared skillet. Place 4–6 blueberries in the pancake.

6 Cook until bubbles appear on the surface, then flip and cook until browned on the other side.

PER SERVING [2 (4-inch) pancakes]

206 Calories	4g Sugar
4g Fat (1g sat)	5g Dietary Fiber
8g Protein	54mg Cholesterol
31g Carbohydrates	267mg Sodium

Asparagus Omelet

Makes 2 servings

½ pound asparagus, trimmed and chopped

1 tablespoon olive oil

2 tablespoons minced shallots

½ pound mushrooms, thinly sliced

3 eggs, lightly beaten

2 egg whites

2 tablespoons milk

¼ teaspoon salt

¼ teaspoon thyme

Dash of freshly ground black pepper

2 tablespoons shredded sharp Cheddar cheese

1. Cut asparagus into 1-inch pieces; cook in boiling water until tender, 2–4 minutes. Drain thoroughly.

2. Heat olive oil in a small skillet. Sauté shallots and mushrooms until wilted and moisture has evaporated. Remove from pan; keep warm.

3. In a small bowl, combine eggs, milk, salt, thyme, and pepper.

4. Lightly coat skillet with cooking spray, and heat skillet to medium high. When hot enough that a drop of water sizzles when dropped in, pour in ½ the egg mixture. Tip pan so eggs coat skillet evenly. As eggs cook, periodically lift up cooked edges, tilt pan and let uncooked egg run underneath.

5. When eggs are cooked, but surface is still shiny, sprinkle 1 tablespoon Cheddar cheese over the top, and layer ½ the asparagus and mushrooms on one side; slide out of pan, folding side without vegetables over top. Repeat for second omelet. Serve immediately.

PER SERVING

274 Calories	0g Sugar
18g Fat (5g sat)	3g Dietary Fiber
19g Protein	328mg Cholesterol
11g Carbohydrates	485mg Sodium

Masala Omelet

Makes 1 serving

During Debra's recent visit to India she enjoyed a Masala Omelet daily along with fresh papaya. We have re-created it here so we could enjoy it at home.

2 eggs

¼ cup chopped tomato

1 tablespoon chopped onion

1 teaspoon chopped fresh cilantro

⅛ teaspoon cumin

¼ teaspoon garam masala powder

1 pinch curry powder

1 teaspoon ghee (clarified butter) or olive oil

Salt and pepper to taste

Garam masala powder is a traditional Indian spice mixture that typically contains coriander, cumin, cardamom, pepper, nutmeg, and cinnamon.

1 Whisk (or beat) the eggs together in a small bowl. Stir in the tomato, onion, cilantro, and spices.

2 Heat medium nonstick skillet over medium heat, and add ghee (alternatively, add olive oil or spray with cooking oil spray) to coat.

3 Add egg mixture, and swirl around to coat bottom of skillet. Stir gently so that eggs begin to set, lifting up one side of eggs to let any residual eggs run underneath.

4 Flip carefully, and cook other side until light brown in color. Season with salt and pepper, if desired.

PER SERVING

202 Calories	0g Sugar
15g Fat (6g sat)	1g Dietary Fiber
13g Protein	436mg Cholesterol
4g Carbohydrates	146mg Sodium

Individual Southwestern Frittatas

Individual Southwestern Frittatas

Makes 4 servings

1 teaspoon olive oil

¼ cup diced red bell pepper

2 tablespoons diced onion

¼ cup canned black beans, drained and rinsed

¼ cup chopped fresh chives

½ ounce shredded Pepper Jack cheese

1 tablespoon minced cilantro

1 dash each: salt, pepper, and paprika

5 large eggs, lightly beaten

1 Preheat oven to 375°. Prepare 4 small individual ramekins by coating lightly with olive oil or cooking oil spray. Alternatively, prepare an oiled muffin tin.

2 Heat oil in a large nonstick skillet over moderately high heat until hot but not smoking, then sauté bell pepper and onion, stirring occasionally, until just tender, about 4 minutes. Stir in black beans.

3 Place a heaping tablespoon of this mixture into the bottom of each ramekin.

4 Whisk chives, cheese, cilantro, salt, pepper, and paprika into eggs. Ladle or spoon egg mixture into ramekins (or prepared muffin tin cups), and bake in middle of oven until tops are puffed and set, about 14 minutes.

5 Remove pan from oven, and serve warm with optional sides of salsa and fresh avocado or fruit.

PER SERVING (1 frittata)

123 Calories	<1g Sugar
8g Fat (2g sat)	1g Dietary Fiber
9g Protein	265mg Cholesterol
4g Carbohydrates	183mg Sodium

Eggs Benedict with Arugula

Makes 4 servings

2 tablespoons unsalted butter

¼ cup half-and-half

2 egg yolks, beaten

2 teaspoons apple cider vinegar

¼ teaspoon salt

¼ teaspoon paprika

½ teaspoon dry mustard

4 eggs

2 whole-wheat English muffins, split and toasted

4 ounces prosciutto

2 cups arugula leaves, rinsed and drained

1 In a small saucepan, melt butter over medium-low heat. Add half-and-half, egg yolks, vinegar, salt, paprika, and mustard; whisk to blend thoroughly.

2 Reduce heat to low, and continue to stir frequently for a few minutes until thickened. Be careful not to overcook, as sauce will curdle.

3 Remove from heat, and then whisk or beat sauce until light and fluffy. Set aside.

4 Poach eggs using conventional poacher or boiling water method.

5 Arrange toasted English muffin halves on serving plates. Layer 1 slice of prosciutto on each of the 4 halves. Divide arugula among the muffin halves on top of prosciutto.

6 Top with 2 tablespoons reserved sauce.

PER SERVING

301 Calories	1g Sugar
18g Fat (12g sat)	2g Dietary Fiber
19g Protein	359mg Cholesterol
15g Carbohydrates	1261mg Sodium

Sweet Potato Hash with Turkey Bacon

Makes 4 servings

1 tablespoon butter

1 teaspoon olive oil

1 medium sweet potato, peeled
  and diced

½ red bell pepper, diced

¼ medium sweet onion, sliced

Salt and pepper to taste

4 slices turkey bacon slices,
  precooked and chopped

1 cup baby spinach

4 large eggs, beaten

Chipotle Hollandaise Sauce,
  page 119 (optional)

1. In a frying pan, melt butter over medium heat. Add olive oil, and sauté sweet potato, bell pepper, sweet onion, and salt and pepper for 3 minutes. Cover; cook over low heat until the potatoes are tender, about 30 minutes.

2. Stir in turkey bacon and spinach, and crack eggs over the top of the mixture. Do not stir. Cover, and cook until eggs are set, about 10 minutes.

3. Scoop ¼ hash mixture plus one egg gently onto plate. Top with Chipotle Hollandaise Sauce, if desired.

PER SERVING

184 Calories	3g Sugar
12g Fat (4g sat)	1g Dietary Fiber
9g Protein	232mg Cholesterol
10g Carbohydrates	288mg Sodium

Tofu Scramble

Makes 4 servings

Delicious with a side of sliced avocado.

2 teaspoons olive oil

⅓ cup diced onion

1 medium carrot, diced

¼ cup diced red bell pepper

½ cup shredded kale

1 small zucchini, diced

14 ounces firm tofu, drained and diced

1 teaspoon tamari soy sauce

¼ teaspoon turmeric powder

¼ teaspoon dried basil

¼ teaspoon dried dill

¼ teaspoon garlic powder

1 tablespoon nutritional yeast (optional)

1 Heat oil in a large nonstick skillet over medium high. Add onion, carrot, and bell pepper, and stir for about 4 minutes.

2 Add kale and zucchini, and stir occasionally for another 3 minutes.

3 Add tofu, tamari, and spices, and continue to cook, stirring, until the tofu begins to brown and the vegetables are just tender.

4 Serve warm.

5 Stir in nutritional yeast, if desired. This lends a nutty flavor and more yellow coloring.

PER SERVING

133 Calories	0g Sugar
7g Fat (1g sat)	2g Dietary Fiber
11g Protein	0mg Cholesterol
10g Carbohydrates	903mg Sodium

Nutritional yeast is a deactivated yeast that is sold commercially in the form of a yellow powder, and can be found in most natural food stores.

Crustless Crab Quiche

Makes 8 servings

1½ cups crabmeat (approximately 8 ounces)

1 cup shredded Swiss cheese

1 cup sliced asparagus, sliced diagonally into ½-inch pieces

½ cup shredded zucchini, drained

⅓ cup diced scallions

5 eggs

1½ cups 1% (skim) milk

¼ teaspoon sea salt

¼ teaspoon lemon pepper

1 dash paprika

1. Preheat oven to 400°. Coat an 11¾ x 7½-inch baking dish with cooking spray.

2. Layer crab, cheese, asparagus, zucchini, and scallions in prepared baking dish.

3. In separate mixing bowl, whisk together eggs, milk, and spices. Pour over layered ingredients in baking dish.

4. Bake 30–40 minutes, or until golden brown and knife inserted in center comes out clean.

5. Allow to stand 5 minutes before serving.

PER SERVING

214 Calories	2g Sugar
16g Fat (2g sat)	2g Dietary Fiber
12g Protein	154mg Cholesterol
7g Carbohydrates	154mg Sodium

Smoked Salmon Quiche

Smoked Salmon Quiche

Makes 6 servings

PASTRY:

1¼ cups Gluten-Free Flour Mixture, page 44 (or whole-wheat pastry flour)

½ teaspoon salt

½ teaspoon sugar

8 tablespoons (1 stick) very cold, unsalted butter, cut into ½-inch cubes

3 tablespoons very cold ice water

FILLING:

1 tablespoon olive oil

½ cup chopped shallots

1 cup chopped spinach leaves

4 large eggs

4 ounces smoked salmon, chopped

3 ounces goat cheese, crumbled

½ cup Greek-style yogurt

½ cup cream

2 tablespoons chopped fresh dill

1 tablespoon chopped fresh chives

1 teaspoon lemon zest

⅛ teaspoon white pepper

1. Preheat oven to 350°. Combine the flour, salt, and sugar in a large bowl. Cut the chilled butter into the dry mixture using a pastry cutter (or alternately, use a food processor). Add the chilled water 1 tablespoon at a time, mixing gently with a fork after each addition. Gently press the dough into a ball; roll out and place in quiche or pie dish.

2. Line Pastry with aluminum foil or parchment paper, pressing into the corners and edges. Fill at least ⅔ full with baking weights (dried beans, rice, etc.).

3. Bake 15 minutes, remove from oven, and let cool a few minutes. Carefully remove aluminum foil and weights.

4. Poke the Pastry with a fork for any air to escape, and return to oven. Bake 10 more minutes, or until lightly golden. Place on a wire rack to cool while making Filling.

5. Heat oil in a small skillet on medium heat. Add the shallots, and cook 2–3 minutes. Add spinach, and stir until wilted.

6. Whisk eggs in a medium bowl; whisk in salmon, goat cheese, yogurt, cream, dill, chives, lemon zest, and pepper.

7. Spoon spinach mixture onto bottom of crust. Pour egg mixture on top.

8. Bake at 350° until just set in the center, 30–35 minutes. Remove from oven, and cool on a wire rack for 15 minutes before serving.

PER SERVING

361 Calories	1g Sugar
32g Fat (18g sat)	trace Dietary Fiber
15g Protein	221mg Cholesterol
4g Carbohydrates	447mg Sodium

Hearty Grains Breakfast

Makes 3 servings

BREAKFAST

1 cup water

¼ cup steel-cut oats

¼ cup brown rice

¼ cup amaranth

½ cup 1% (skim) milk

1 ounce currants

¼ teaspoon ground cinnamon

1 ounce chopped pecans

2 tablespoons ground flax

1　Put water in a large saucepot along with steel-cut oats, rice, and amaranth. Bring to a boil, then stir, and reduce heat to a simmer. Maintain at a low simmer for 25 minutes, stirring frequently.

2　Add the milk to the oat/rice mixture, and stir.

3　Add the currants and cinnamon. Stir gently to combine, and cook for an additional 10 minutes or until most of the liquid evaporates and grains are wonderfully chewy.

4　Stir in the chopped pecans and ground flax.

PER SERVING

350 Calories	9g Sugar
10g Fat (1g sat)	10g Dietary Fiber
11g Protein	2mg Cholesterol
49g Carbohydrates	31mg Sodium

Yogurt Parfait

Makes 1 serving

6 ounces plain Greek-style yogurt

½ cup blueberries

¼ tablespoon granola

¼ teaspoon fresh-grated lemon zest for garnish

1 Alternate layers of yogurt, blueberries, and granola in a beautiful bowl or glass flute.

2 Garnish with a light sprinkling of fresh-grated lemon zest.

PER SERVING

178 Calories	14g Sugar
4g Fat (3g sat)	2g Dietary Fiber
18g Protein	15mg Cholesterol
19g Carbohydrates	103mg Sodium

Granola

Makes about 15 servings

6 cups rolled oats

½ cup sliced almonds

½ cup chopped walnuts

½ cup chopped macadamia nuts

⅓ cup canola oil

⅓ cup maple syrup

1 teaspoon maple extract

1 teaspoon cinnamon

1. Preheat oven to 325°.

2. Stir together all of the ingredients in a large bowl, making sure to coat all of the oats evenly.

3. Pour onto 2 sheet pans (lining them with parchment will make clean up a bit easier). Cook for about 30 minutes, stirring every 10 minutes to achieve an even color.

4. Remove from oven, and transfer into a large bowl or storage container (wait until cool to seal).

PER SERVING (½ cup)

271 Calories	4.9g Sugar
15g Fat (2g sat)	4g Dietary Fiber
8g Protein	0mg Cholesterol
29g Carbohydrates	3mg Sodium

Dr. James Rouse

Pasta

Broccoli and Chicken Whole-Wheat Rotini

Broccoli and Chicken Whole-Wheat Rotini

Makes 4 servings

2 cups cooked whole-wheat rotini pasta

2 cups cooked broccoli

1 tablespoon olive oil

12 ounces chopped, cooked chicken breasts (about 2 cups)

2 tablespoons pine nuts

¼ cup shredded Parmesan cheese

Salt and pepper to taste

1 Cook pasta according to directions.

2 Lightly steam broccoli and set aside.

3 When pasta is done, drain water, return to pot, and stir in olive oil.

4 Add broccoli, chicken, and pine nuts, and toss.

5 Divide into 4 serving bowls, and top each with 1 tablespoon shredded Parmesan and salt and pepper to taste.

PER SERVING

321 Calories	1g Sugar
13g Fat (3g sat)	6g Dietary Fiber
30g Protein	62mg Cholesterol
23g Carbohydrates	165mg Sodium

Chicken Primavera Pasta Salad

Makes 6 servings

6 ounces rotini

8 ounces cooked chicken, chopped

1 medium red bell pepper, seeded and diced

½ cup pitted and chopped olives, mix of green and kalamata

3 ounces chopped spinach

2 tablespoons olive oil

¼ cup lemon juice

1½ teaspoons grated lemon peel

¾ teaspoon crushed dried basil

¾ teaspoon crushed dried oregano

1 ounce grated Parmesan cheese

Salt and pepper to taste

1 Cook rotini according to package directions. Drain, and return to cooking pot.

2 Add cooked chicken, bell pepper, olive, and spinach, and stir gently until well combined.

3 In a small bowl, whisk together olive oil, lemon juice and peel, and herbs. Toss with pasta mixture. Sprinkle in Parmesan cheese, and toss again.

4 Serve at room temperature or chilled.

PER SERVING

257 Calories	2g Sugar
9g Fat (2g sat)	2g Dietary Fiber
18g Protein	36mg Cholesterol
25g Carbohydrates	229mg Sodium

PASTA

Dr. James Rouse

Chicken Ratatouille Pasta

Makes 4 servings

2 cups whole-wheat penne pasta

2 tablespoons olive oil

½ cup diced onion

1 cup diced eggplant

1 cup diced green bell pepper

1 cup diced red bell pepper

1 cup diced zucchini

1 (14½-ounce) can fire roasted diced tomatoes

⅛ teaspoon salt

⅛ teaspoon pepper

1 tablespoon chopped fresh basil

2 cups cooked shredded rotisserie chicken breast

¼ cup grated Parmesan cheese

1 Cook pasta according to package directions; drain.

2 While pasta is cooking, heat a large saucepan over medium-high heat. Add oil, onion, eggplant, and bell peppers. Cook, stirring frequently, until veggies are wilted and lightly caramelized.

3 Add zucchini, and cook about 3 more minutes or until tender, stirring frequently. Add tomatoes, salt, pepper, fresh basil, and shredded chicken. Stir well.

4 Spoon hot ratatouille mixture over pasta. Sprinkle with grated Parmesan.

PER SERVING (with Parmesan cheese)

449 Calories	7g Sugar
11g Fat (2g sat)	5g Dietary Fiber
38g Protein	73mg Cholesterol
50g Carbohydrates	562mg Sodium

To make a vegetarian version, leave out the chicken; for a vegan version, leave out the chicken and cheese.

Pistachio Cilantro Pesto Chicken Spaghetti

Pistachio Cilantro Pesto Chicken Spaghetti

Makes 4 servings

8 ounces whole-wheat spaghetti

¼ cup extra virgin olive oil

1 cup chopped fresh cilantro leaves, loosely packed, washed

1 small shallot, chopped

1 tablespoon minced ginger

½ cup shelled, unsalted pistachio nuts

Salt and freshly ground pepper to taste

½ pound boneless skinless chicken breast, cooked, shredded or chopped

¼ cup chopped olives

Shredded Asiago cheese (optional)

1 Cook pasta according to package directions; drain well.

2 Blend/purée olive oil, cilantro, shallot, ginger, pistachio nuts, salt and pepper in food processor.

3 Toss pasta with half the "pesto" dressing.

4 Add chicken and olives, and toss again.

5 Top with a tablespoon of Asiago cheese, if desired.

PER SERVING (without Asiago cheese)

504 Calories	0g Sugar
25g Fat (4g sat)	3g Dietary Fiber
25g Protein	33mg Cholesterol
46g Carbohydrates	131mg Sodium

Gluten-Free Spaghetti and Meatballs

Makes 6 servings

1 (12-ounce) package brown rice spaghetti

1 pound ground chicken breast

1 medium egg white

2 tablespoons (gluten-free) bread crumbs*

1 cup chopped spinach, (if using frozen spinach, thaw and drain excess moisture)

1 dash each: salt and pepper

¼ teaspoon dried oregano

1 tablespoon olive oil

1 medium shallot, diced

½ medium yellow onion, diced

1 medium garlic clove, chopped

1 (28-ounce) can diced fire roasted tomatoes

½ teaspoon dried basil

½ teaspoon dried oregano

1 dash hot sauce

⅛ teaspoon each: salt and pepper

Grated pecorino cheese (optional)

* For gluten-free bread crumbs, toast a piece of gluten-free bread, then blend it in a food processor. This recipe can also be made using store-bought bread crumbs and whole-grain or regular spaghetti.

1 Preheat oven to broil. Line a rimmed baking pan with parchment paper or aluminum foil, lightly coated with cooking oil spray.

2 Cook spaghetti according to package directions until al dente. Most gluten-free (rice-based) spaghetti will take 13–17 minutes. Drain, and reserve.

3 Mix together ground chicken, egg white, bread crumbs, drained spinach, salt, pepper, and oregano in a medium bowl. Form into walnut-size balls, and place on prepared baking pan.

4 Broil the meatballs in oven for 8 minutes, then carefully rotate, and broil for another 8 minutes.

5 While the meatballs are cooking, heat olive oil in a large skillet over medium-high heat. Add shallot and onion, and stir frequently for about 5 minutes, reducing heat to medium. Add garlic, tomatoes, basil, oregano, hot sauce, salt, and pepper. Stir well, and simmer on low.

6 When done, gently add each meatball to the skillet with the tomato sauce. Add drained spaghetti noodles; toss to coat. Serve immediately with pecorino cheese, if desired.

PER SERVING

242 Calories	2g Sugar
4g Fat (trace fat)	2g Dietary Fiber
5g Protein	trace Cholesterol
48g Carbohydrates	121mg Sodium

Dr. James Rouse

Linguine Alfredo Primavera

Makes 4 servings

8 ounces whole-grain linguine

1 tablespoon olive oil

¼ cup chopped onion

2 cups chopped broccoli florets

1 cup chopped baby spinach

1 clove garlic, minced

SAUCE:

1 cup 2% milk

½ cup grated low-sodium Parmesan cheese

¼ teaspoon each: salt and pepper

½ cup chopped fresh parsley

1 Cook pasta in 3-quart saucepan according to package directions. Drain, and return to saucepan.

2 Heat olive oil in a large saucepan; add onion and broccoli, stir, and cook on medium high for about 4 minutes.

3 Add spinach and garlic, and stir until spinach is wilted.

4 In a medium saucepan, bring the milk to a simmer, and stir in Parmesan cheese, salt, and pepper. As soon as the cheese has melted, and the Sauce is creamy, pour into vegetable mixture.

5 Add linguine noodles and fresh parsley, and stir until well combined.

6 Serve warm.

PER SERVING

323 Calories	3.5g Sugar
9g Fat (3g sat)	6g Dietary Fiber
16g Protein	12mg Cholesterol
50g Carbohydrates	374mg Sodium

Cajun Chicken Fettuccine

Makes 6 servings

12 ounces whole-grain fettuccine

¾ pound boneless skinless chicken breasts, pounded flat and sliced thin

3 teaspoons olive oil, divided

1 tablespoon unsalted butter

1 tablespoon Cajun seasoning

½ cup chopped onion

½ cup chopped celery

1 medium red bell pepper (about ⅔ cup), cored, seeded, and chopped

1½ tablespoons lemon juice

1 teaspoon dried thyme

1 teaspoon dried oregano

½ cup low-sodium chicken broth

½ teaspoon cornstarch

½ cup grated Parmesan cheese

1 Cook pasta according to package directions.

2 While pasta is cooking, sauté chicken breast slices in 1 teaspoon of olive oil and butter, and sprinkle with Cajun seasoning. Cook, and stir over medium heat until browned and cooked through, about 4 minutes.

3 Remove the chicken from pan, and keep warm.

4 Add onion, celery, and pepper to pan along with remaining 2 teaspoons of olive oil. Sauté until crisp-tender.

5 Stir in lemon juice, thyme, oregano, chicken broth, and cornstarch. Heat until sauce begins to simmer. Then turn off heat, and continue to stir until everything is well mixed.

6 When pasta is done, drain well. Toss pasta and reserved chicken with sauce; top with Parmesan cheese.

PER SERVING

361 Calories	1g Sugar
8g Fat (3g sat)	3g Dietary Fiber
25g Protein	43mg Cholesterol
47g Carbohydrates	326mg Sodium

Seafood Pasta

2 tablespoons rice vinegar

1 tablespoon hoisin sauce*

2 cloves garlic, minced

2 teaspoons minced fresh ginger

1 teaspoon olive oil

1 teaspoon sesame oil

1 tablespoon fresh orange zest

2 tablespoons chopped fresh cilantro

½ pound small bay scallops

½ pound medium fresh shrimp, peeled and deveined (tail removed)

12 ounces whole-grain pasta (bow ties, rotini, udon noodles)

1½ cups snow peas

1 teaspoon cornstarch

1 tablespoon water

1 Combine the vinegar, hoisin sauce, garlic, ginger, olive oil, sesame oil, orange zest, and fresh cilantro in a nonmetallic bowl; add shrimp and scallops, and toss gently to coat seafood. Cover, and refrigerate 30 minutes to an hour, stirring occasionally.

2 Cook pasta according to directions on package. Drain, and return to cooking pot.

3 Heat oil in a nonstick wok or skillet; add shrimp and scallop mixture (do not drain). Stir-fry 2 minutes.

4 Add snow peas, cover, and cook 2 minutes or until shrimp are pink and scallops are opaque.

5 Dissolve cornstarch in water; stir into skillet. Cook about a minute.

6 Stir pasta into seafood mixture. Serve hot.

PER SERVING

319 Calories	2g Sugar
3g Fat (trace sat)	2g Dietary Fiber
22g Protein	70mg Cholesterol
48g Carbohydrates	166mg Sodium

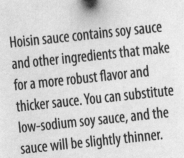

Hoisin sauce contains soy sauce and other ingredients that make for a more robust flavor and thicker sauce. You can substitute low-sodium soy sauce, and the sauce will be slightly thinner.

Spring Pizza

Spring Pizza

Makes 5 servings

Nothing beats the taste of a homemade crust, but if you're rushed for time, you can purchase a prepared crust and simply skip to the Toppings. When you prepare the Crust using a stand mixer, food processor, or breadmaker, it simplifies the kneading process tremendously.

CRUST: (or use prepared crust)

1 teaspoon yeast

1 cup very warm water (110°–120°)

1 teaspoon honey

2 tablespoons olive oil, divided

½ teaspoon sea salt

1½ cups all-purpose flour

1½ cups whole-wheat flour, divided

Extra flour for dusting kneading surface

1 teaspoon cornmeal

TOPPINGS:

2–3 tablespoons marinara sauce (or sub tomato or pizza sauce)

½ cup shredded fontina cheese

½ cup shredded mozzarella cheese

2 tablespoons grated Romano and/or Parmesan cheese

2 cups chopped asparagus

1 cup chopped green beans

2 tablespoons diced shallots

1. Add yeast to warm water and honey, and whisk together. Add 1 tablespoon olive oil and salt; stir briefly, and allow to rest about 5 minutes.

2. Add the all-purpose flour and 1 cup whole-wheat flour to the yeast mixture. Attach the mixer bowl and the dough "hook" attachment to the mixer, and mix on a low setting for about a minute.

3. Add remaining ½ cup flour, and mix until the dough comes away from the sides of the mixing bowl and begins to stick slightly around the dough hook.

4. Briefly knead dough on a clean, lightly floured surface until smooth and elastic, about a minute. Place in an oiled bowl, cover, and let rise for 30–50 minutes.

5. Roll out dough to desired size and thickness. Sprinkle with cornmeal and brush with remaining olive oil. Top with desired amount of marinara, tomato sauce, or pizza sauce. Sprinkle evenly with cheeses.

6. Add asparagus, green beans, and shallots. (Lightly stir-fry in a teaspoon of olive oil and a little salt and pepper, if desired.)

7. Preheat oven and pizza baking stone (or cookie sheet) to 450°. Cook pizza for about 15 minutes or until the crust is lightly browned and cheese has melted.

PER SERVING (2 pieces)

423 Calories	2.5g Sugar
13g Fat (5g sat)	8g Dietary Fiber
18g Protein	20mg Cholesterol
62g Carbohydrates	404mg Sodium

Penne Rigate with Shrimp and Veggies

Makes 6 servings

PASTA

2 cups chopped cauliflower flowerets

1 medium red onion, peeled and cut into 1-inch-thick wedges

2 cups chopped broccoli florets

2 tablespoons red wine vinegar

¼ cup extra virgin olive oil

2 garlic cloves, minced

1 teaspoon oregano

1 teaspoon thyme

1 dash each: salt and pepper, or to taste

1 pound large shrimp, rinsed, peeled, and deveined

12 ounces whole-wheat penne rigate

1 teaspoon olive oil

1 teaspoon unsalted butter

½ cup chopped fresh parsley

⅓ cup grated Parmesan cheese

1 Preheat oven to 500°. Prepare a large rimmed baking pan by lining with parchment or foil.

2 Bring a large pot of salted water to a boil. Add cauliflower, onion, and broccoli to the pot. Blanch for about 1 minute. Drain, reserving cooking water for pasta.

3 Whisk together vinegar, olive oil, garlic, oregano, thyme, salt, and pepper in a medium bowl. Add vegetables and shrimp, and toss until well coated.

4 Pour mixture onto prepared baking pan. Roast for about 15 minutes until shrimp is cooked through, stirring once or twice while they are roasting.

5 While the veggies and shrimp are in the oven, return the pot of water to a boil. Add penne, and cook according to package directions. Drain, and return to pot.

6 Toss penne with olive oil and butter. Add veggie and shrimp mixture, and toss again.

7 Garnish with fresh parsley and grated Parmesan.

PER SERVING

224 Calories	<1g Sugar
13g Fat (3g sat)	2g Dietary Fiber
19g Protein	120mg Cholesterol
7g Carbohydrates	245mg Sodium

Salads

Arugula Salad with Scallops and Basil

Arugula Salad
with Scallops and Basil

Makes 4 servings

4 tablespoons extra virgin olive oil, divided

1½ tablespoons fresh lemon juice

1½ tablespoons balsamic vinegar

2 teaspoons grainy mustard

1 teaspoon sugar or honey

½ teaspoon sea salt, divided

10 cups arugula

1 cup chopped fresh basil leaves

½ cup roasted tomatoes

1 pound large scallops

¼ cup grated Asiago cheese

Freshly ground pepper to taste

1 Whisk 3 tablespoons oil, lemon juice, vinegar, mustard, sugar, and ¼ teaspoon salt in a small bowl.

2 Combine arugula, basil, and tomatoes in a large bowl.

3 Sprinkle scallops with remaining salt. Heat remaining oil in a large nonstick skillet over high heat. Add scallops and cook, turning or tossing from time to time just until they turn pink and are opaque in the center, 2–3 minutes.

4 Meanwhile, whisk the dressing again, and pour over arugula mixture; toss to coat.

5 Divide salad mixture onto 4 plates.

6 Add scallops on top, and sprinkle with a tablespoon of cheese on each salad. Grind on pepper to taste.

PER SERVING

420 Calories	2.5g Sugar
19g Fat (3g sat)	8g Dietary Fiber
31g Protein	44mg Cholesterol
40g Carbohydrates	753 Sodium

Salmon Niçoise Salad

Makes 4 servings

1 head Bibb lettuce

1 cup green beans, lightly cooked and cooled

1 large tomato, sliced into wedges

1 small red bell pepper, thinly sliced

½ cup thinly sliced red onion

3 tablespoons olive oil

3 tablespoons white wine vinegar

½ teaspoon dry mustard

1 clove garlic, minced

8 ounces cooked wild salmon (boneless and skinless)

4 medium hard-boiled eggs, peeled and halved

1½ tablespoons capers

1 Wash and dry lettuce. Tear leaves into bite-size pieces.

2 Add lettuce to a large mixing bowl, and toss together with the beans, tomato, red bell pepper, and red onion.

3 In another bowl, whisk together olive oil, vinegar, mustard, and garlic.

4 Divide salad onto 4 plates, and top with 2 ounces of cooked salmon (you can use fresh grilled, canned, or smoked).

5 Arrange 2 hard-boiled egg halves on each side of the plate and sprinkle a teaspoon of capers over the salad.

6 Drizzle vinaigrette evenly over the salad just prior to serving.

PER SERVING

283 Calories	2g Sugar
19g Fat (4g sat)	3g Dietary Fiber
19g Protein	243mg Cholesterol
9g Carbohydrates	413mg Sodium

Steak Salad

Makes 6 servings

1½ pounds flank steak

Salt and pepper to taste

8 ounces mixed greens

BASIC VINAIGRETTE:

2 tablespoons red or white balsamic vinegar

1 tablespoon red wine vinegar

1 tablespoon Dijon mustard

1 tablespoon chopped shallot

1 garlic clove, minced

½ cup olive oil

1 Start with a clean grill. Brush grates with a bit of olive oil prior to heating. Preheat grill to medium high.

2 Season steak on both sides with salt and pepper. Grill steak to desired doneness, about 5 minutes per side for medium rare. Remove from heat, and allow to rest for 5 minutes before slicing.

3 Toss greens in large bowl with 6 tablespoons Basic Vinaigrette. Divide onto 6 serving plates.

4 Thinly slice steak across grain on slight diagonal. Arrange steak atop greens.

5 For vinaigrette, whisk together vinegars, mustard, shallot, and garlic.

6 Add the oil in a slow steady stream, whisking constantly.

7 Season with salt and pepper to taste.

8 Refrigerate any unused portions. Serve at room temperature.

PER SERVING (salad)

377 Calories	0g Sugar
30g Fat (7g sat)	2g Dietary Fiber
23g Protein	58mg Cholesterol
4g Carbohydrates	98mg Sodium

PER SERVING (1 tablespoon dressing)

82 Calories	0g Sugar
9g Fat (1g sat)	trace Dietary Fiber
trace Protein	0mg Cholesterol
1g Carbohydrates	16mg Sodium

Baby Bok Choy Salad

Baby Bok Choy Salad

Makes 4 servings

3 tablespoons olive oil

1 tablespoon sesame oil

2 tablespoons rice vinegar

1 tablespoon sugar or honey

1 tablespoon tamari soy sauce

3 bunches bok choy, cleaned and sliced

4 green onions, chopped

½ cup shredded carrots

8 ounces cooked chicken breast, chopped

1 Whisk together olive oil, sesame oil, vinegar, sugar, and tamari soy sauce.

2 Combine bok choy, green onions, carrots, and chicken in a medium serving bowl.

3 Toss with prepared dressing, and serve.

PER SERVING

244 Calories	3.25g Sugar
17g Fat (3g sat)	1g Dietary Fiber
15g Protein	39mg Cholesterol
8g Carbohydrates	326mg Sodium

For a vegan version, leave out the chicken, and use sugar or agave, instead of honey.

Turkey Taco Salad

Makes 4 servings

1 tablespoon safflower oil

1 pound lean ground turkey

¼ cup diced white onion

2 teaspoons chili powder, or to taste

¼ teaspoon garlic powder

¼ teaspoon cumin powder

¼ cup paprika

2 tablespoons low-sodium chicken broth

1 head romaine lettuce, shredded

2 tomatoes, diced

1 cup pinto beans, or black beans

½ cup shredded Cheddar cheese

Baked tortilla chips (optional)

1 Add safflower oil to a heavy skillet, and heat over medium heat.

2 Stir in ground turkey, and brown lightly.

3 Stir in onion, chili powder, garlic powder, cumin, and paprika.

4 Add broth, and stir again. Simmer uncovered until most of the liquid evaporates, about 10 minutes, stirring occasionally.

5 Prepare 4 salad bowls with about a cup of shredded lettuce each.

6 Spoon ½ cup turkey mixture onto the lettuce.

7 Sprinkle ¼ cup diced tomatoes, pinto beans, and 2 tablespoons Cheddar cheese on top.

8 Serve with a small side of baked corn chips or additional lettuce, if desired.

PER SERVING

573 Calories	1g Sugar
30g Fat (11g sat)	18g Dietary Fiber
36g Protein	81mg Cholesterol
44g Carbohydrates	211mg Sodium

Dr. James Rouse

Summer Salad

¾ cup chopped fresh strawberries

6 cups torn red leaf lettuce

¼ cup chopped cashews

¼ cup chopped green onions

POPPYSEED DRESSING:

½ cup white vinegar

¼ cup honey

¼ teaspoon salt

1 teaspoon dry mustard

1 green onion, white part only, minced

1 cup safflower or olive oil

1 tablespoon poppyseeds

1. Add chopped strawberries, lettuce, chopped cashews, and green onions to a large bowl; toss to combine.

2. Drizzle with Poppyseed Dressing.

3. For Poppyseed Dressing, combine the vinegar, honey, salt, mustard, green onion, and oil in a blender or food processor. Blend for about 20 seconds.

4. Pour into a serving container, and stir in poppyseeds.

5. Refrigerate any unused portions. Serve at room temperature.

PER SERVING (salad)

72 Calories	1g Sugar
4g Fat (1g sat)	3g Dietary Fiber
3g Protein	0mg Cholesterol
8g Carbohydrates	10mg Sodium

PER SERVING (1 tablespoon dressing)

165 Calories	4.5g Sugar
16g Fat (1g sat)	trace Dietary Fiber
trace Protein	0mg Cholesterol
6g Carbohydrates	39mg Sodium

Warm Spinach Sweet Potato Salad

Warm Spinach Sweet Potato Salad

Makes 4 servings

2 medium sweet potatoes, cubed

4–5 cups torn fresh spinach

1 tablespoon olive oil

½ cup sliced mushrooms

1 red bell pepper, chopped

1 garlic clove, minced

2 bacon slices, cooked, drained, and crumbled

Salt and pepper to taste

HONEY MUSTARD VINAIGRETTE:

¼ cup red wine vinegar

2 tablespoons honey or agave nectar

2 teaspoons Dijon mustard

1 clove garlic, minced

1 teaspoon chopped shallot

¼ teaspoon each: salt and pepper

1 teaspoon minced fresh ginger

⅓ cup olive oil

1 Preheat oven to 375°. Prepare a large baking sheet by coating lightly with cooking oil spray.

2 Wash and scrub sweet potatoes. Cut into 1-inch or smaller cubes. Add to a large bowl. Coat lightly with olive oil spray. Toss to coat. Spread out over prepared baking sheet. Bake for about 30 minutes or until lightly browned on the outside and tender. Set aside to cool slightly.

3 Wash and stem spinach, tearing leaves into small pieces. Place in a large bowl, and set aside.

4 Heat oil in a frying pan over medium-high heat. Add mushrooms and red bell pepper, and cook until mushrooms start to sweat and bell peppers soften. Add garlic, and cook until transparent.

5 Spoon hot vegetable mixture over spinach. Add cooked sweet potatoes and bacon crumbles, and toss well.

6 Drizzle with ¼ cup Honey Mustard Vinaigrette.

7 Whisk or blend all Honey Mustard Vinaigrette ingredients together. Refrigerate any unused portions. Serve at room temperature.

PER SERVING (salad)

479 Calories	4g Sugar
7g Fat (2g sat)	2g Dietary Fiber
95g Protein	256mg Cholesterol
4g Carbohydrates	319mg Sodium

PER SERVING (1 tablespoon dressing)

65 Calories	2.5g Sugar
6g Fat	trace Dietary Fiber
trace Protein	0mg Cholesterol
3g Carbohydrates	40mg Sodium

Fennel Cucumber Tomato Salad

Makes 4 servings

1 medium cucumber, chopped

2 medium tomatoes, chopped

½ cup thinly sliced fennel

¼ cup thinly sliced red onion

¼ cup crumbled feta cheese

1 tablespoon balsamic vinegar

2 tablespoons olive oil

Salt and pepper to taste

1 Combine ingredients, and toss to coat evenly.

PER SERVING

115 Calories	1.5g Sugar
9g Fat (2g sat)	2g Dietary Fiber
3g Protein	8mg Cholesterol
7g Carbohydrates	118mg Sodium

Dr. James Rouse

Greek Salad

Makes 5 servings

Serve with vinaigrette of your choice.

3 medium tomatoes

1 pound romaine lettuce

1 medium cucumber, sliced or diced

2½ ounces crumbled feta cheese

½ medium red onion, sliced into rings

2 ounces pitted and chopped kalamata olives

1 Toss together all of the ingredients, and divide onto 5 servings plates.

PER SERVING (without vinaigrette)

210 Calories	3g Sugar
17g Fat (4g sat)	3g Dietary Fiber
5g Protein	13mg Cholesterol
11g Carbohydrates	438mg Sodium

Broccoli Slaw

Makes 4 servings

½ tablespoon rice wine vinegar

½ teaspoon sesame oil

1 teaspoon olive oil

¼ teaspoon salt

½ teaspoon sugar

1 cup broccoli slaw

½ cup shredded carrots

1 tablespoon chopped fresh cilantro

1 tablespoon chopped fresh mint

1 In a bowl, combine vinegar, oils, salt, and sugar.

2 Add broccoli slaw, shredded carrots, cilantro, and mint; toss and serve.

PER SERVING

48 Calories	3g Sugar
3g Fat (trace sat)	1g Dietary Fiber
trace Protein	0mg Cholesterol
4g Carbohydrates	408mg Sodium

Mediterranean Chopped Veggie Salad

Mediterranean Chopped Veggie Salad

Makes 4 servings

We make many versions of this scrumptious summertime salad. This is our favorite.

2 red bell peppers

2 yellow bell peppers

1 small red onion

2 large portobello mushroom caps

1 zucchini

1 small eggplant

2 tablespoons olive oil, divided

Salt and pepper to taste

2 tablespoons crumbled feta cheese

¼ cup chopped pitted black olives

½ cup chopped marinated artichoke hearts

1 tablespoon red wine (or balsamic) vinegar

1 Thoroughly wash all the vegetables, removing seeds and stems from the peppers, and drying so that there isn't a lot of water left on the surface.

2 Cut the peppers, onion, and mushroom into quarters, and slice the zucchini and eggplant lengthwise into about 4 or 5 slices. (They are easier to grill or roast this way.)

3 Lightly coat the vegetables with 1 tablespoon of olive oil. Sprinkle lightly with salt and pepper. Roast in the oven on a broiling pan, or grill them.

4 After grilling, allow the vegetables to cool. Then chop them and place in a large mixing bowl.

5 Add the feta cheese, olives, and artichoke hearts, and toss until well combined.

6 Drizzle remaining 1 tablespoon of olive oil and red wine vinegar over the salad, and toss it together.

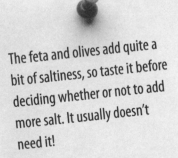

The feta and olives add quite a bit of saltiness, so taste it before deciding whether or not to add more salt. It usually doesn't need it!

PER SERVING (about 1 cup)

151 Calories	1g Sugar
7g Fat (1g sat)	5g Dietary Fiber
5g Protein	4mg Cholesterol
19g Carbohydrates	229mg Sodium

Asparagus Salad

Makes 4 servings

1 tablespoon white balsamic vinegar

1 teaspoon red wine vinegar

½ teaspoon sea salt

1 teaspoon honey

1 teaspoon Dijon mustard

2 tablespoons olive oil

1 teaspoon sesame oil

1½ pounds fresh asparagus, trimmed and cut into 2-inch pieces

1 tablespoon sesame seeds

1 Whisk together the vinegars, salt, honey, and mustard. Drizzle in the olive oil and sesame oil while whisking vigorously to emulsify. Set aside.

2 Bring a pot of lightly salted water to a boil. Add the asparagus to the water, and cook 3–5 minutes until just tender, but still mostly firm. Remove and rinse under cold water to stop from cooking any further.

3 Place the asparagus on a serving platter, and drizzle with half the dressing. Sprinkle with sesame seeds to serve.

4 Serve additional dressing on the side in a small serving bowl.

PER SERVING

128 Calories	1g Sugar
9g Fat (1g sat)	4g Dietary Fiber
4g Protein	0mg Cholesterol
10g Carbohydrates	254mg Sodium

Curried Shrimp Salad with Honeydew

Makes 4 servings

¼ cup plain yogurt

1 tablespoon low-fat mayonnaise

1 tablespoon curry powder

1 tablespoon fresh lime juice

1½ teaspoons peeled and minced fresh ginger

1 pound cooked medium shrimp, deveined and shells removed

½ cup thinly sliced sweet onion

¼ cup chopped macadamia nuts (optional)

8 cups mixed salad greens

½ honeydew melon, seeded and thinly sliced (into 12 slices)

1 Combine first 5 ingredients in medium bowl, and mix well.

2 Add shrimp, and toss until coated.

3 Toss onion, nuts, and greens together.

4 Add shrimp mixture to the greens mixture, and toss until everything is lightly coated.

5 Serve on chilled salad plates with 3 slices of honeydew on the side.

PER SERVING

675 Calories	13g Sugar
45g Fat (7 sat)	18g Dietary Fiber
15g Protein	28mg Cholesterol
65g Carbohydrates	438mg Sodium

Chopped Chicken Salad

Chopped Chicken Salad

Makes 4 servings

8 cups romaine lettuce, chopped

½ pound cooked chicken breast, chopped

2 ounces salami, cut into thin strips

2 ounces mozzarella cheese, cut into small cubes or strips

½ cup cherry tomatoes, chopped into quarters

¼ cup chopped scallions

1 medium avocado, pitted and chopped

¼ cup Cilantro Vinaigrette

CILANTRO VINAIGRETTE:

1 cup chopped fresh cilantro, packed

1 tablespoon chopped fresh ginger

1 tablespoon chopped shallots

1 clove fresh garlic, minced

1 teaspoon sea salt

¼ cup red wine vinegar

½ cup olive oil

¼ cup grapeseed or canola oil

2 tablespoons water

1 Add lettuce, chicken, salami, mozzarella, cherry tomatoes, scallions, and avocado to a large bowl.

2 Toss with ¼ cup of Cilantro Vinaigrette, and add more as desired.

3 Purée all Cilantro Vinaigrette ingredients together in a blender until smooth.

4 Refrigerate any unused portions. Serve at room temperature.

PER SERVING (includes dressing)

297 Calories	3g Sugar
20g Fat (6g sat)	4g Dietary Fiber
23g Protein	62mg Cholesterol
8g Carbohydrates	372mg Sodium

Edamame Salad

Edamame and all preparations of soybeans are rich in carbohydrates, protein, dietary fiber, and micronutrients, particularly folates, manganese, and vitamin K. Choose organic soybean products whenever possible since most conventional soy products have been genetically modified.

½ cup cooked pinto beans

1½ cups cooked brown rice

1 cup edamame

½ medium avocado, chopped

½ medium red bell pepper, chopped

1 medium tomato, seeded and chopped

¼ tablespoon chopped scallions

2 tablespoons chopped fresh cilantro

2 teaspoons fresh lime juice

1 tablespoon grapeseed oil

1 dash each: salt and pepper

1 In a medium mixing bowl, combine beans, rice, edamame, avocado, red bell pepper, tomato, and scallions. Toss until well combined.

2 Add cilantro, lime juice, grapeseed oil, salt, and pepper, and toss again until well coated.

PER SERVING

265 Calories	5g Sugar
11g Fat (1g sat)	7g Dietary Fiber
11g Protein	0mg Cholesterol
33g Carbohydrates	55mg Sodium

SALADS

Vegetables & Sides

Grilled Summer Vegetables

Grilled Summer Vegetables

3 tablespoons olive oil

1 tablespoon red wine vinegar

2 garlic cloves, chopped

1½ teaspoons chopped fresh rosemary

⅛ teaspoon each: salt and pepper

1 small eggplant, sliced into 1-inch thick rounds

2 medium zucchini, sliced lengthwise into ¼-inch slices

2 medium yellow squash, sliced lengthwise into ¼-inch slices

6 slices red onion (½ inch thick)

2 medium red bell peppers, quartered, seeded

1 Whisk together olive oil, vinegar, garlic, rosemary, salt, and pepper.

2 Place vegetables in large bowl, pour marinade on top, and toss until well coated. Cover, and let marinate at least one hour to overnight.

3 Heat grill to medium high, around 400°. Grill until just tender, 4–5 minutes each side.

4 Transfer vegetables to platter, and serve warm or at room temperature.

PER SERVING

170 Calories	6g Sugar
7g Fat (1g sat)	7g Dietary Fiber
4g Protein	0mg Cholesterol
25g Carbohydrates	41mg Sodium

VEGETABLES & SIDES

Baked Sweet Potato Slices

Makes 4 servings

This is one of our favorite side dishes—a great alternative to fries!

3 medium sweet potatoes,
  scrubbed and sliced about ¼ inch
  thick
2 tablespoons olive oil
½ teaspoon cumin
½ teaspoon cinnamon
½ teaspoon sea salt
½ teaspoon paprika
½ teaspoon pepper

1 Preheat oven to 375°. Prepare 9x13-inch baking dish by coating lightly with cooking oil spray.

2 Add sliced sweet potatoes to a large mixing bowl, and drizzle with olive oil. Toss until sweet potatoes are lightly coated with oil.

3 Combine spices in a small bowl, stirring together until well mixed. Add to sweet potatoes, and toss until seasoning is well distributed over the sweet potatoes.

4 Bake for 35 minutes, stirring once so that they are evenly cooked.

PER SERVING

165 Calories	1g Sugar
7g Fat (1g sat)	3g Dietary Fiber
2g Protein	0mg Cholesterol
24g Carbohydrates	248mg Sodium

Brussels Sprouts with Fingerling Potatoes

Makes 4 servings

12 ounces Brussels sprouts (about 2 cups)

12 ounces fingerling potatoes,* mixed colors (12–15 potatoes)

2 medium shallots, chopped

1 tablespoon olive oil

1 tablespoon melted unsalted butter

2 tablespoons sweet red chili sauce (available in Asian section of supermarket)

⅛ teaspoon salt

⅛ teaspoon pepper

*If you cannot find multi-colored fingerling potatoes, you can substitute baby red potatoes or yellow fingerlings.

1 Preheat oven to 375°. Prepare a deep sided baking dish by coating with cooking spray.

2 Wash Brussels sprouts and potatoes well. Trim bottoms and outer leaves from Brussels sprouts, then slice in half vertically, and place in large bowl. Chop potatoes into small bite-size pieces, and add to bowl with sprouts.

3 Add chopped shallots to bowl, and toss everything together.

4 Combine melted butter, olive oil, and sweet red chili sauce, and stir until well combined. Drizzle on top of vegetable mixture, and toss well to coat. Sprinkle with salt and pepper, and toss again.

5 Add mixture to prepared baking dish. Bake for 30 minutes or until potatoes are soft on the inside and Brussels sprouts have started to brown.

PER SERVING

181 Calories	3.25g Sugar
7g Fat (2g sat)	4g Dietary Fiber
5g Protein	8mg Cholesterol
28g Carbohydrates	145mg Sodium

New Red Potatoes with Feta and Walnuts

Makes 4 servings

8 ounces new red potatoes, chopped into ¾-inch pieces

½ cup chopped olives

1 ounce chopped walnuts

1 ounce crumbled feta cheese

½ cup thinly sliced fennel

2 tablespoons chopped fresh cilantro

3 tablespoons vinaigrette of your choice

1 Boil potatoes in salted water until soft, approximately 10 minutes. Drain, and let cool.

2 Add potatoes to medium bowl. Mix in olives, walnuts, feta, fennel, and cilantro.

3 Drizzle in vinaigrette, and toss until everything is well coated.

PER SERVING

182 Calories	1.5g Sugar
13g Fat (3g sat)	2g Dietary Fiber
4g Protein	6mg Cholesterol
13g Carbohydrates	236mg Sodium

We list generic vinaigrette here because this versatile side dish can take on many flavors. We like to use Honey Mustard Vinaigrette (page 91).

Roasted Asparagus with Balsamic Vinegar

Makes 4 servings

1¼ pounds asparagus spears (about 20 spears)

2 teaspoons olive oil

⅛ teaspoon sea salt

2 tablespoons finely chopped shallots

1 teaspoon balsamic vinegar

1 Preheat oven to 400°. Rinse asparagus spears, and break off tough ends.

2 Toss asparagus with olive oil, salt, shallots, and vinegar.

3 Bake on a baking sheet or ceramic baking dish for 15 minutes.

4 Serve hot or at room temperature.

PER SERVING

41 Calories	1g Sugar
2g Fat (trace sat)	2g Dietary Fiber
2g Protein	0mg Cholesterol
4g Carbohydrates	61mg Sodium

Harvest Casserole

Harvest Casserole

Makes 8 servings

6 medium red potatoes (about 1½ pounds)

1 cup lentils (you can also substitute lean ground beef)

2 cups low-sodium vegetable broth

1 large onion, chopped

2 large carrots, roughly chopped

2 tablespoons olive oil

½ cup frozen green peas

2 cloves garlic, minced

½ teaspoon thyme or rosemary

¼ teaspoon sea salt

¼ teaspoon pepper

½ cup 2% milk

2 tablespoons butter or olive oil

½ cup grated Parmesan cheese

1 dash cayenne pepper (optional)

PER SERVING

245 Calories	3g Sugar
8g Fat (3g sat)	10g Dietary Fiber
14g Protein	13mg Cholesterol
30g Carbohydrates	341mg Sodium

1 Scrub and wash potatoes. Cook in boiling water for about 25 minutes until tender. Drain well, and set aside.

2 Pick over lentils to remove any debris. Rinse and drain the lentils, then add them to a medium pot with broth. Bring to a boil for a few minutes, then reduce heat and simmer until tender, about 30 minutes. If the lentils are not fully soft, add a bit of water, and cook until soft.

3 Meanwhile, sauté onion and carrots in olive oil until the onions are translucent and the carrots start to become tender, about 10 minutes.

4 Remove from heat, then stir in green peas, garlic, thyme, salt, and pepper. Add lentils.

5 Preheat oven to 350° and prepare a medium casserole dish (3- to 3½-quart) by coating with cooking oil spray.

6 Mash or whip potatoes; add milk, butter (or oil), and cheese. For additional spice, add salt, pepper, and a dash of cayenne, if desired. Blend until fluffy.

7 Transfer lentil mixture to casserole dish. Spread mashed potatoes evenly on top.

8 Bake for 15 minutes or until potato mixture starts to brown and form a crust.

Cauliflower Curry

Makes 4 servings

1 tablespoon olive oil

¼ pound baby red potatoes, cut into small cubes (about 3 small potatoes)

1 sweet onion, chopped

¼ cup low-sodium vegetable broth (plus a few tablespoons more, if needed)

1 clove garlic, minced

1 tablespoon minced fresh ginger

1 tablespoon curry powder

1 small cauliflower head, cut into bite-sized pieces

Salt and pepper to taste

¼ cup chopped fresh cilantro or basil

1 Heat olive oil in a large skillet over medium-high heat. Add potatoes, and stir for about 3 minutes. Add chopped onion, and continue to stir for another 2 minutes. Add broth, cover, and lower heat to low for about 5 minutes or until potatoes become tender.

2 Remove cover, and stir in garlic, ginger, and curry powder. Add cauliflower, and stir until well mixed. Cover again for 5 minutes. If necessary, add a bit more broth or water so that cauliflower will become lightly steamed.

3 Season to taste with salt and pepper. Make sure potatoes have softened before serving. Garnish with fresh cilantro or basil.

PER SERVING

109 Calories	2g Sugar
4g Fat (1g sat)	5g Dietary Fiber
5g Protein	0mg Cholesterol
16g Carbohydrates	80mg Sodium

Sautéed Kale with Almonds

Makes 4 servings

2 tablespoons olive oil

1 clove garlic, minced

1 teaspoon minced fresh ginger

¼ cup sliced almonds

1½ pounds kale or chard, washed, trimmed from stem, and cut into 1-inch pieces

2 tablespoons low-sodium chicken or vegetable broth

1 tablespoon tamari soy sauce

Feel free to substitute any greens in this recipe—its a great way to use up beet greens, spinach, collards, etc. You may need to adjust the seasonings accordingly.

1 Heat a large nonstick skillet over medium-high heat. Add olive oil, garlic, and ginger, and sauté for about 30 seconds.

2 Add almonds, and stir-fry about 1 minute before adding kale.

3 Add kale, broth, and tamari soy sauce. Sauté, and stir about 5 minutes or until kale is wilted but not soggy.

PER SERVING

204 Calories	<1g Sugar
13g Fat (2g sat)	4g Dietary Fiber
8g Protein	0mg Cholesterol
19g Carbohydrates	342mg Sodium

Roasted Broccoli with Parmesan

Makes 5 servings

2½ pounds broccoli

3 tablespoons olive oil, divided

2 garlic cloves, chopped

2 tablespoons pine nuts

1 teaspoon sea salt

½ teaspoon pepper

1 pinch red pepper flakes

2 teaspoons lemon zest

¼ cup grated Parmesan cheese

1 Preheat oven to 425°.

2 Cut bite-sized florets of broccoli from the stalk, and cut the top inch of the stalk into small rounds, about ⅛ inch thick. Add broccoli to a large bowl, and drizzle with 2 tablespoons olive oil.

3 Add garlic, pine nuts, salt, pepper, and red pepper flakes, and toss again.

4 Spread broccoli mixture out onto a large sheet pan (save mixing bowl for when it comes out of the oven). Roast for about 15 minutes, checking at 10–12 minutes to make sure broccoli isn't getting too brown.

5 Remove from oven, and return to mixing bowl.

6 Toss right away with remaining tablespoon olive oil, lemon zest, and Parmesan. Serve hot.

PER SERVING

151 Calories	<1g Sugar
12g Fat (2g sat)	4g Dietary Fiber
7g Protein	3mg Cholesterol
9g Carbohydrates	488mg Sodium

Herb-Roasted Tomatoes

Makes 5 servings

1½ pounds plum tomatoes, halved lengthwise (stem removed)

2 tablespoons olive oil

¼ teaspoon salt

¼ teaspoon black pepper

1 teaspoon dried oregano

½ tablespoon finely chopped basil

½ teaspoon finely chopped thyme

½ teaspoon finely chopped rosemary

1 Preheat oven to 375°.

2 Place tomatoes cut side up in a 9x13-inch pan. Brush with olive oil.

3 Sprinkle tomatoes lightly with salt and pepper.

4 Mix herbs together in a small bowl. Sprinkle herb mixture over tomatoes.

5 Bake tomatoes until tender and slightly browned around the edges, about 35 minutes.

PER SERVING

74 Calories	3.5g Sugar
6g Fat (1g sat)	1g Dietary Fiber
1g Protein	0mg Cholesterol
6g Carbohydrates	118mg Sodium

Stuffed Red Bell Peppers

Stuffed Red Bell Peppers

Makes 4 servings

2 medium red bell peppers

1 tablespoon olive oil

1 medium leek, washed and chopped

¼ cup diced red bell pepper

1 cup finely chopped broccoli, stalk and florets

¼ cup pine nuts

1 cup cooked brown rice

1 ounce Gouda cheese

1 ounce smoked chinook salmon, diced or chopped

Salt and pepper to taste

1 Preheat oven to 375°. Prepare a large baking sheet by lining with parchment or aluminum foil.

2 Slice red bell peppers in half horizontally, and remove seeds and ribs. Place on prepared baking sheet.

3 Heat olive oil in a large skillet, and add leek and diced red bell pepper. Sauté on medium high for about 4 minutes, stirring regularly.

4 Add broccoli and pine nuts, and continue to stir another 2 minutes. Stir in brown rice.

5 At this stage you can either stir the Gouda and the salmon into the skillet (one less thing to clean), or you can scoop the other ingredients into a large bowl and stir in the Gouda and salmon.

6 Place about ⅓ cup of the mixture into each red bell pepper half.

7 Bake peppers for about 35 minutes. Serve warm.

PER SERVING

204 Calories	3g Sugar
11g Fat (3g sat)	4g Dietary Fiber
8g Protein	10mg Cholesterol
21g Carbohydrates	125mg Sodium

Inspired Vegetarian Casserole

Makes 4 servings

1 tablespoon olive oil

1 stalk celery, trimmed and diced

¾ cup diced sweet onion

1 cup seeded and chopped red bell pepper

1 cup seeded and chopped yellow bell pepper

2 garlic cloves, minced

¼ jalapeño pepper, diced

1 teaspoon ground cumin

1 teaspoon oregano

2 tablespoons low-sodium vegetable or chicken broth

1 cup cooked black beans

1 cup canned pinto beans

1 cup cooked brown rice

½ cup shredded Cheddar cheese

Cilantro and sour cream for garnish (optional)

1 Preheat oven to 350°.

2 Heat olive oil in a large oven-proof skillet (cast-iron works well) over medium-high heat. Add celery, onion, and bell peppers, and stir for 3–4 minutes.

3 Stir in garlic, jalapeño, cumin, and oregano. Add broth, and stir again for about 3 more minutes. Turn off stove.

4 Add beans and rice to vegetable mixture, and stir until well combined. Sprinkle Cheddar cheese over the top. Place skillet in oven.

5 Bake for 25 minutes. Serve warm.

6 Garnish with chopped cilantro and sour cream, if desired.

PER SERVING

193 Calories	1.5g Sugar
6g Fat (2g sat)	6g Dietary Fiber
9g Protein	10mg Cholesterol
27g Carbohydrates	247mg Sodium

Sauces & Dressings

Grape Tomato Salsa

Makes 1⅓ cups (4 servings)

We add a little bit of olive oil to encourage absorption of lycopene from the tomatoes. Lycopene is a fat-soluble antioxidant that may help protect against certain forms of cancer.

1 pint cherry tomatoes, cut in half

¼ medium jalapeño pepper, seeded and diced (or more, for spicier salsa)

1 garlic clove, chopped

¼ cup chopped onion

¼ teaspoon olive oil

1 tablespoon lime juice

¼ cup chopped cilantro

⅛ teaspoon salt

⅛ teaspoon pepper

1 The quickest and easiest way to make this salsa is to roughly chop all of the ingredients, and then add them to the bowl of a food processor fitted with the S blade. Then pulse to chop to desired consistency.

2 Refrigerate until ready to use.

PER SERVING (⅓ cup)

30 Calories	2g Sugar
1g Fat (trace)	1g Dietary Fiber
1g Protein	0mg Cholesterol
6g Carbohydrates	78mg Sodium

Teriyaki Sauce

Makes about 1¾ cups (28 servings)

1 cup low-sodium tamari soy sauce

½ cup sesame oil

3 tablespoons brown sugar

3 garlic cloves, pressed or minced

2 tablespoons grated fresh ginger

2 tablespoons sherry

1 Combine all ingredients in an airtight jar with lid, and shake well to combine (or blend).

2 Refrigerate until ready to use.

PER SERVING (1 tablespoon)

40 Calories	1.5g Sugar
3g Fat (1g sat)	trace Dietary Fiber
trace Protein	0mg Cholesterol
2g Carbohydrates	300mg Sodium

Chipotle Hollandaise

Makes ½ cup (8 servings)

¼ cup unsalted butter, melted

3 medium egg yolks

2 tablespoons boiling hot water

1 chipotle chile (chopped), canned in adobo, plus 1 teaspoon sauce

1 tablespoon lime juice

Salt and pepper to taste (no more than ⅛ teaspoon each)

1 Melt butter in a small saucepan over low heat, being careful not to brown or burn.

2 In a medium bowl, beat together egg yolks and hot water until yolks are just starting to thicken. Add chipotle chile, sauce, and lime juice, and continue to beat.

3 Slowly beat in the melted butter, and season with salt and pepper.

4 Cover with plastic wrap or foil, and allow to sit for about 5 minutes to continue to thicken.

5 Refrigerate until ready to use.

Note: For a speedy version of this recipe, melt the butter in a nonmetal bowl in a microwave. Add yolks, water, chiles, and lime juice to a blender, and blend on medium high for about 30 seconds. Then slowly add the butter while continuing to blend on low (assuming your blender has a pouring spout, if not, just add in a few batches, and cover between blending so you don't spatter hollandaise). Season to taste with salt and pepper.

PER SERVING (1 tablespoon)

74 Calories	0g Sugar
8g Fat (4g sat)	trace Dietary Fiber
1g Protein	95mg Cholesterol
trace Carbohydrates	15mg Sodium

Green Goddess Avocado Dressing

Makes 1½ cups (12 servings)

2 tablespoons chopped shallots

3 tablespoons chopped fresh basil

1½ tablespoons chopped fresh ginger

1 tablespoon tamari soy sauce

1 tablespoon honey or agave

¼ cup white balsamic vinegar

¾ cup olive oil (up to 1 cup)

1 tablespoon lemon juice

½ medium avocado

2 tablespoons water

1 Combine all ingredients in a blender, and blend until smooth. If a thinner dressing is desired, you can dilute with water.

2 Refrigerate until ready to use. Serve at room temperature.

PER SERVING (2 tablespoons)

142 Calories	1g Sugar
15g Fat (2g sat)	trace Dietary Fiber
trace Protein	0mg Cholesterol
3g Carbohydrates	51mg Sodium

Greek-Style Ranch Dressing

Makes 1 cup (8 servings)

½ cup Greek-style yogurt

⅓ cup 2% milk

2 teaspoons lemon juice

2 tablespoons mayonnaise

1 tablespoon Dijon mustard

1 tablespoon minced shallots

1 tablespoon chopped fresh dill

2 tablespoons chopped fresh chives

⅛ teaspoon sea salt

⅛ teaspoon pepper

1 Add all ingredients to food processor fitted with S blade. Process until well blended and smooth.

2 Carefully pour into small receptacle for serving.

3 Refrigerate until ready to use. Serve at room temperature.

PER SERVING (2 tablespoons)

45 Calories	2g Sugar
4g Fat (1g sat)	trace Dietary Fiber
2g Protein	3mg Cholesterol
2g Carbohydrates	87mg Sodium

Dr. James Rouse

Soups, Stews, & Chili

Chicken Vegetable Soup

Chicken Vegetable Soup

Makes 4 servings

1 tablespoon olive oil

1 medium onion, diced

1 large carrot, sliced

1 large stalk celery, sliced

¾ pound boneless skinless chicken breasts, cut into ¾-inch cubes

1½ cups diced tomatoes, or 1 (15-ounce) can diced tomatoes

½ cup chopped zucchini

½ cup chopped broccoli

½ cup chopped green beans

6 cups reduced-sodium chicken broth

1 teaspoon dried thyme leaves, crushed

Salt and pepper to taste (optional)

2 tablespoons chopped fresh parsley

1 Sauté olive oil, onion, carrot, and celery to a large stockpot over medium high, and stir until onions are translucent.

2 Add chicken, and continue to cook until chicken is nearly cooked.

3 Add diced tomatoes, zucchini, broccoli, green beans, broth, and thyme. Bring to a boil, reduce heat to low, and cover.

4 Cook for an additional 10 minutes; season with salt and pepper, if desired.

5 Garnish with parsley. Serve warm.

PER SERVING

243 Calories	3.5g Sugar
5g Fat (1g sat)	3g Dietary Fiber
38g Protein	49mg Cholesterol
13g Carbohydrates	857mg Sodium

White Bean and Barley Soup

1 cup cannellini beans, soaked overnight

2 tablespoons extra virgin olive oil

2 large stalks celery and leafy tops, chopped

1 medium onion, chopped

1 clove garlic, minced

3 cups low-sodium chicken or vegetable broth

6 cups water

½ cup barley, or short-grain brown rice

2 medium carrots, chopped

½ teaspoon oregano

½ teaspoon basil

⅛ teaspoon pepper

¼ cup chopped fresh parsley (optional)

1 (28-ounce) can tomatoes

Salt to taste

1 Soak beans overnight in filtered water. Discard the water, and rinse the beans.

2 Heat oil in large saucepan; add celery, onion, and garlic. Sauté 2–3 minutes. Add liquids, beans, barley, carrots, oregano, basil, and pepper. Simmer 1–1½ hours or until beans are tender.

3 Add parsley, if desired, and tomatoes, breaking them up with a fork. Heat 10 minutes over high heat or until hot. Season with salt, if desired.

PER SERVING

306 Calories	5g Sugar
7g Fat (1g sat)	12g Dietary Fiber
14g Protein	0mg Cholesterol
51g Carbohydrates	289mg Sodium

Dr. James Rouse

Hungarian Mushroom Soup

Makes 6 servings

2 tablespoons butter

1 tablespoon olive oil

2 cups cremini mushrooms, cleaned and thinly sliced

1 cup shiitake mushrooms, cleaned and chopped

2 cups chopped onions

8 ounces Neufchâtel cream cheese, softened

3 tablespoons dill weed

1 tablespoon Hungarian (or smoked) paprika

1 tablespoon tamari soy sauce

4 cups low-sodium vegetable broth

3 teaspoons fresh lemon juice

½ teaspoon sea salt

½ teaspoon black or white pepper

1 Add butter and olive oil to a large stockpot, and set on medium-high heat.

2 Add mushrooms and onions, and sauté until heated through and onions are translucent.

3 Reduce heat, and stir in cream cheese, dill, paprika, and tamari until you get a creamy consistency.

4 Add vegetable broth, and stir until well incorporated.

5 Add the lemon juice, salt, and pepper.

PER SERVING

338 Calories	2g Sugar
16g Fat (8g sat)	8g Dietary Fiber
17g Protein	39mg Cholesterol
40g Carbohydrates	870mg Sodium

Curried Butternut Squash & Apple Soup

Makes 6 servings

SOUPS, STEWS, & CHILI

1 medium onion, chopped

2 tablespoons butter

2 tablespoons minced fresh
gingerroot

2 tablespoons curry powder

4 cups low-sodium vegetable broth

1 pound butternut squash, peeled,
seeded, and chopped

2 Granny Smith apples, peeled,
seeded, and chopped

¼ teaspoon salt

¼ teaspoon white pepper

OPTIONAL GARNISHES:

6 tablespoons crème fraîche

1 Granny Smith apple, peeled,
seeded, and thinly sliced

½ cup toasted chopped pecans

1 Cook and stir onion in butter in 4-quart stockpot until tender.

2 Add ginger and curry, and stir for another few minutes.

3 Add broth, squash, and apples. Heat to boiling; reduce heat to low. Cover, and simmer until squash is tender, 15–20 minutes.

4 Purée about half of the soup in a food processor or covered blender until smooth. (Be conscious of soup temperature and careful with your equipment.) Repeat with remaining soup. Return to stockpot.

5 Season with salt and pepper to taste. Heat, stirring frequently, until hot.

6 If desired, top each serving with a tablespoon dollop of crème fraîche, and garnish with sliced apples and pecans.

PER SERVING (garnishes not included)

244 Calories	7.5g Sugar
14g Fat (6g sat)	6g Dietary Fiber
10g Protein	24mg Cholesterol
22g Carbohydrates	485mg Sodium

Dr. James Rouse

Kale Soup

1 medium onion, coarsely chopped

2 tablespoons olive oil

2 medium carrots, diced

2 garlic cloves, minced

5 cups low-sodium vegetable or chicken broth

1 cup water

2 tablespoons tomato paste

1 pinch cayenne pepper

1 teaspoon finely chopped fresh rosemary

½ pound kale, stems and center ribs removed, leaves coarsely chopped

2 cups cooked white beans, or 1 (16-ounce) can

Salt and pepper to taste

⅓ cup grated Parmesan cheese (optional)

1 Add onion and olive oil to a large stockpot and sauté over medium high.

2 Stir in the carrots, and cook for 5 minutes.

3 Lower heat to medium; stir in the garlic, being careful not to let it brown.

4 Add the broth, water, tomato paste, cayenne, and rosemary, and stir until well combined.

5 Add the kale and the white beans, and simmer over low heat until the kale is tender, about 15 minutes. Season with salt and pepper to taste.

6 Let rest for a few hours before serving. Then re-warm on the stovetop, and serve topped with a small sprinkle of freshly grated Parmesan, if desired.

PER SERVING

227 Calories	<1g Sugar
6g Fat (2g sat)	9g Dietary Fiber
19g Protein	3mg Cholesterol
26g Carbohydrates	587mg Sodium

SOUPS, STEWS, & CHILI

Gazpacho

Gazpacho

2 cups diced tomatoes

1 green bell pepper, medium dice

1 red bell pepper, medium dice

1 medium cucumber, peeled, seeded, medium dice

1 tablespoon chopped jalapeño chile pepper

2 medium scallions, diced

1 tablespoon honey

½ cup diced red onion

1 clove garlic, minced

1 tablespoon red wine vinegar

1 tablespoon fresh lime juice

2 cups vegetable juice, divided

1 tablespoon olive oil

Salt and pepper to taste

Fresh basil for garnish

1 Combine first 11 ingredients (tomatoes through lime juice) in a large bowl, and toss well to mix.

2 Purée half of the tomato mixture in a blender or food processor with 1 cup of vegetable juice. Return the puréed mixture to the other ingredients.

3 Stir in the remaining vegetable juice plus olive oil, and season with salt and pepper, if desired.

4 Garnish with fresh basil.

PER SERVING

85 Calories	5.5g Sugar
3g Fat (trace sat)	3g Dietary Fiber
2g Protein	0mg Cholesterol
15g Carbohydrates	304mg Sodium

SOUPS, STEWS, & CHILI

Tomatillo Chicken Stew

Makes 6 servings

3 tablespoons olive oil, divided

1 pound boneless skinless chicken breasts, cut into 1-inch cubes

1 onion, chopped

2 cloves garlic, minced

1 pound tomatillos, chopped

1 (15-ounce) can diced tomatoes, no salt added

1 (4-ounce) can diced green chiles

1 medium jalapeño pepper, seeded and minced

4 cups low-sodium chicken broth

½ teaspoon ground cumin

¼ teaspoon cayenne pepper

2 tablespoons chopped fresh cilantro

Salt and pepper to taste

¼ cup sour cream, or Greek-style yogurt (optional)

1 Heat 2 tablespoons olive oil in a large soup pot over medium-high heat. Add chopped chicken, and stir-fry until lightly browned, approximately 4 minutes. Remove the chicken, and set aside.

2 To the same pot, add remaining 1 tablespoon oil along with onion and garlic, and sauté until golden.

3 Stir in the tomatoes, diced green chiles, jalapeño pepper, broth, cumin, and cayenne. Bring to a boil. Reduce heat, cover the pot, and simmer for about 15 minutes.

4 Purée tomatillo mixture in batches in a blender or food processor. Return to pot, and reheat.

5 Add the chicken into the soup. Stir in fresh cilantro. Season to taste with salt and pepper.

6 Serve with a dollop of sour cream or plain Greek-style yogurt, if desired.

PER SERVING

238 Calories	5g Sugar
11g Fat (3g sat)	2g Dietary Fiber
26g Protein	48mg Cholesterol
10g Carbohydrates	427mg Sodium

Lentil Vegetable Stew

1 large onion, chopped (about 1 cup)

½ cup chopped fresh parsley

2 cloves garlic, finely chopped

1 teaspoon ground cinnamon

½ teaspoon ground turmeric

½ teaspoon pepper

¼ teaspoon minced gingerroot

2 tablespoons olive oil

4 cups low-sodium vegetable broth, divided

2 medium carrots, diced

1 cup dried lentils, sorted and rinsed

1 cup brown rice, uncooked

1 (15-ounce) can diced tomatoes

2 cups water

1 cup sliced green beans (fresh or frozen)

½ teaspoon sea salt

½ teaspoon pepper

¾ cup organic Greek-style yogurt

3 sprigs mint, chopped

1. In a Dutch oven or large skillet, sauté onion, parsley, garlic, cinnamon, turmeric, pepper, and ginger in olive oil, stirring occasionally, until onion is tender.

2. Stir in 3 cups broth, carrots, lentils, and rice. Heat to boiling; reduce heat. Cover, and simmer 25 minutes.

3. Stir in tomatoes and additional cup of broth and water (½ cup at a time). Heat to boiling; reduce heat. Cover, and simmer 20 minutes.

4. Stir in green beans. Cover, and simmer about 15 minutes or until beans, lentils, and rice are all tender. Season with salt and pepper.

5. You can partially purée the mixture with an immersion blender, or serve as is.

6. Garnish with a dollop of yogurt on top and a sprinkle of fresh mint.

PER SERVING

363 Calories	4g Sugar
7g Fat (1g sat)	16g Dietary Fiber
23g Protein	3mg Cholesterol
55g Carbohydrates	546mg Sodium

SOUPS, STEWS, & CHILI

Not Just for Diabetics   131

Turkey Cherry Chili

Makes about 8 servings

2 cups low-sodium chicken broth, divided (you can also use 1 cup water and 1 cup broth)

½ cup unsweetened dried tart cherries

1 tablespoon olive oil

1 cup chopped onion

1 medium red bell pepper, seeded and diced

1 pound ground turkey

½ medium jalapeño chile pepper, seeded and finely chopped

1 teaspoon garlic powder

2 teaspoons chili powder

1½ teaspoons ground cumin

1 teaspoon ground coriander

½ teaspoon dried oregano

2 (16-ounce) cans fire roasted diced tomatoes

2 cups cooked black beans

¼ cup chopped fresh cilantro

1 In a small saucepan, heat 1 cup of the broth. Add cherries, turn off heat, and set aside.

2 Heat olive oil in a large stockpot over medium heat. Add onion and red bell pepper; sauté until onion is soft, about 5 minutes.

3 Add turkey; cook until no longer pink.

4 Stir in jalapeño; cook 1 minute.

5 Stir in spices, and cook another few minutes.

6 Add tomatoes, beans, and remaining broth; bring to a boil. Reduce heat; simmer, uncovered, about 5 minutes.

7 Stir in cilantro. Continue cooking until thoroughly heated.

PER SERVING

216 Calories	5g Sugar
7g Fat (2g sat)	5g Dietary Fiber
17g Protein	45mg Cholesterol
22g Carbohydrates	193mg Sodium

Sandwiches & Wraps

Fancy Grilled Cheese

Fancy Grilled Cheese

1 tablespoon olive oil

1 dash each: salt and pepper

1 dash chopped rosemary

2 medium whole-grain sandwich flats (or thin bun)

2 tablespoons chèvre cheese or cream cheese

1 large tomato, thinly sliced

½ medium sweet onion, thinly sliced

½ cup arugula, washed and patted dry

1 ounce shredded Monterey Jack cheese

1 ounce shredded Cheddar cheese

1 Combine the olive oil with salt, freshly ground pepper, and rosemary. Brush the olive oil mixture over the outside of each sandwich flat.

2 On the inside of one slice of each sandwich flat, spread 1 tablespoon of chèvre cheese. Top with 2 slices of tomato, 1 slice of onion, ¼ cup of arugula and half the shredded Monterey Jack and Cheddar cheese (about 2 tablespoons each). Top with other half of sandwich flat.

3 Prepare a large nonstick skillet or panini press, and heat over medium-high heat. Carefully place sandwiches on hot skillet.

4 Cook the sandwich for about 3 minutes on each side. Press down with spatula if you like a flatter sandwich. Sandwich is done when cheese is melted and both sides of bread or bun are golden. If your bread is browning too quickly, turn down heat on the skillet.

PER SERVING (1 sandwich)

607 Calories	3g Sugar
22g Fat (9g sat)	5g Dietary Fiber
21g Protein	34mg Cholesterol
81g Carbohydrates	1,051mg Sodium

SANDWICHES & WRAPS

Chicken Salad Sandwich

Makes 4 servings

2 cups shredded or chopped cooked chicken

2 stalks celery, finely chopped

½ cup red grapes, sliced in half

2 tablespoons diced red onion

2 tablespoons mayonnaise

1 tablespoon Dijon mustard

¼ cup Greek-style yogurt

2 teaspoons fresh lemon juice

⅛ teaspoon salt

1 dash white pepper

2 tablespoons chopped fresh tarragon

8 slices French bread or whole-grain bread

2 cups mesclun salad mix

1 Chop or shred chicken coarsely. Add to medium bowl along with celery, grapes, and red onion.

2 In another bowl, combine mayonnaise, mustard, yogurt, lemon juice, salt, pepper, and tarragon. Stir well.

3 Add chicken mixture to mayonnaise mixture, and stir well to coat.

4 Divide mixture onto 4 pieces of bread, top with ½ cup mesclun salad, then top with second slice of bread.

PER SERVING (1 sandwich)

341 Calories	5.5g Sugar
11g Fat (2g sat)	2g Dietary Fiber
28g Protein	63mg Cholesterol
32g Carbohydrates	538mg Sodium

Dr. James Rouse

Olive Egg Salad Sandwich

6 medium eggs, hard-boiled

2 tablespoons finely chopped scallions

⅓ cup diced celery

1 tablespoon diced kalamata olives

¼ cup diced sweet onion

¼ cup Greek-style yogurt

2 teaspoons Dijon mustard

¼ cup red wine vinegar

1 dash paprika

1 dash celery salt

1 dash each: salt and pepper

3 slices whole-grain bread

1 Peel, rinse, and dice eggs, and add to medium mixing bowl.

2 Add scallions, celery, olives, and sweet onion, and stir to mix.

3 Add yogurt, mustard, vinegar, paprika, celery salt, and salt and pepper; stir well until all ingredients are thoroughly "dressed."

4 Serve open face on toasted whole-grain bread.

PER SERVING

294 Calories	1g Sugar
14g Fat (4g sat)	4g Dietary Fiber
19g Protein	426mg Cholesterol
25g Carbohydrates	631mg Sodium

For lower "carb" option, serve atop mixed greens.

SANDWICHES & WRAPS

Pork and Slaw Hoagies

Pork and Slaw Hoagies

1 recipe Slow Cooked Pork
(page 166)

1 recipe Broccoli Slaw (page 93)

4 hoagie rolls

1 Split hoagie rolls in half. Scoop ¼ cup of pork onto half of hoagie.

2 Top with ¼ cup broccoli slaw.

PER SERVING (1 hoagie)

499 Calories	5g Sugar
19g Fat (5g sat)	4g Dietary Fiber
31g Protein	53mg Cholesterol
51g Carbohydrates	1700mg Sodium

Sunflower Burgers

2 cups sunflower seeds

1 cup cooked brown rice

½ cup grated carrots

1 teaspoon parsley

1 teaspoon salt

1 teaspoon sage

1 teaspoon black pepper

1 Add all ingredients to food processor and process until chunky, paste-like consistency develops.

2 Divide mixture evenly into 6 patties (about ½ cup mixture per patty).

3 Brown patties on both sides in a lightly oiled or nonstick skillet. You may also choose to cook the patties in a 350° oven for about 20 minutes.

VARIATIONS: Add 2 eggs to the mixture, topping with cheese, or add ½ cup grated cheese to the mixture.

PER SERVING (1 patty)

394 Calories	0 Sugar
25g Fat (3g sat)	6g Dietary Fiber
13g Protein	0mg Cholesterol
34g Carbohydrates	362mg Sodium

SANDWICHES & WRAPS

Black Bean Burgers

SANDWICHES & WRAPS

1 (15-ounce) can black beans
1 tablespoon horseradish mustard
2 tablespoons tomato paste
1 tablespoon flour
1 teaspoon ground cumin
1 tablespoon olive oil
¼ cup minced onion
1 garlic clove, minced
¼ cup chopped shiitake mushrooms
1 piece whole-wheat bread, toasted
2 tablespoons almonds

1 Drain black beans of any liquid, and place in a medium bowl. Mash with a fork, and add mustard, tomato paste, flour, and cumin.

2 Meanwhile, add olive oil to a medium-hot skillet. Add onion, garlic, and mushrooms, and sauté about 5 minutes or until mushrooms are tender. Add to black bean mixture, and stir until well mixed.

3 In a toaster or warm oven, toast whole-wheat bread until it dries out but isn't burnt. Tear bread into pieces, and process with almonds in a food processor or coffee grinder until well ground. Dip each black bean patty into the bread/almond mixture on each side.

4 Cook patties on medium high in a skillet coated with cooking spray. Cook each side 3–4 minutes or until desired doneness.

5 Serve each patty on salad greens, a whole-wheat bun, or an English muffin.

PER SERVING (1 burger)

281 Calories	2g Sugar
7g Fat (1g sat)	13g Dietary Fiber
13g Protein	0mg Cholesterol
45g Carbohydrates	163mg Sodium

Salmon Burgers

Makes 4 servings

2 small cans wild salmon (boneless, skinless, about 6 ounces each)

2 tablespoons lemon juice

1½ teaspoons Dijon mustard

¾ cup bread crumbs

½ cup sliced green onions

2 eggs

1 Place all ingredients into a food processor, and pulse until well blended, but not liquid.

2 Form mixture into 4 patties, and grill or broil until golden brown on each side and heated through.

3 Serve each burger on a bun with lettuce, tomato slices, and condiments as desired.

4 Serve atop a bed of mixed greens, or on a bun with lettuce, tomato slices, and condiments as desired.

PER SERVING (1 patty)

241 Calories	1.5g Sugar
8g Fat (2g sat)	1g Dietary Fiber
25g Protein	57mg Cholesterol
17g Carbohydrates	807mg Sodium

Turkish Burgers

Turkish Burgers

Makes 4 servings

1 pound ground turkey breast or thighs

¼ cup pitted and diced kalamata olives

1 teaspoon dried parsley

¼ teaspoon dried thyme

½ teaspoon garlic powder

¼ teaspoon cinnamon

⅛ teaspoon nutmeg

½ teaspoon salt

¼ teaspoon pepper

RED PEPPER SAUCE:

1 cup chopped roasted red pepper

¼ cup feta cheese

¼ teaspoon garlic powder

1 pinch chopped fresh rosemary

The preparation can be quite messy, so if you prefer, you can simply make the burgers and top with the Red Pepper Sauce.

1 In medium bowl, combine turkey, olives, parsley, thyme, garlic powder, cinnamon, nutmeg, salt, and pepper. Form into 8 very thin burgers, about 3 inches in diameter. Cover, and refrigerate.

2 For Red Pepper Sauce, add roasted peppers, feta, garlic powder, and rosemary to a blender or food processor, and blend or purée until smooth.

3 Spoon 1 teaspoon Red Pepper Sauce onto middle of 4 burger patties. Place other burger patties on top of the sauce, and carefully press sides together to form 4 burgers.

4 Cook on medium-high heat on grill or in a skillet. Cook on each side for at least 4 minutes, until turkey is no longer pink in the center.

5 Serve with additional Red Pepper Sauce and a sliced tomato over a bed of greens, or in your favorite whole-grain bun.

PER SERVING (1 stacked patty)

214 Calories	1.5g Sugar
12g Fat (4g sat)	1g Dietary Fiber
22g Protein	98mg Cholesterol
3g Carbohydrates	553mg Sodium

Spicy Turkey Burgers

Makes 4 servings

1 pound ground turkey

⅓ cup quick-cooking oats

½ cup salsa, divided

¼ cup finely chopped shallots

¼ cup chopped cilantro

1 teaspoon Worcestershire

1 tablespoon finely chopped chipotle chiles canned in adobo

1 teaspoon cumin powder

½ teaspoon salt

¼ teaspoon pepper

¼ cup shredded chèvre cheese (feel free to substitute favorite cheese, smoked mozzarella is good here)

1 Combine turkey and oats in a large bowl. Add ½ the salsa along with the other ingredients, and mix thoroughly.

2 Form mixture into 8 flat patties. Place 1 tablespoon of chèvre cheese on 4 of the patties. Top with second patty and press sides together so that you have 4 "stuffed" turkey patties.

3 Grill on preheated grill at medium-high for 5–7 minutes per side.

4 Serve "naked" or with whole-grain buns, sliced tomato, and onion. Top with remaining salsa.

PER SERVING (1 stacked patty)

232 Calories	0g Sugar
10g Fat (3g sat)	2g Dietary Fiber
27g Protein	77mg Cholesterol
10g Carbohydrates	544mg Sodium

Turkey and Smoked Gouda Panini

Makes 2 servings

½ cup shredded smoked Gouda cheese

2 teaspoons mayonnaise

2 teaspoons mustard

¼ teaspoon garlic powder

4 slices whole-wheat bread, crusts removed and toasted

¼ pound sliced deli turkey (nitrate free)

4 slices tomato

½ medium avocado, ripe

2 romaine leaves

1 In a small bowl, combine the cheese, mayonnaise, mustard, and garlic powder.

2 Spread 2 slices of bread with cheese mixture, turkey, tomato, avocado, and romaine. Top with remaining bread.

3 Spray the tops of each piece of bread with olive oil cooking spray. Use a panini press or heat a skillet on the stove over medium heat. Place sandwiches on press or skillet, and cook for about 4 minutes on each side.

PER SERVING (1 sandwich)

409 Calories	2g Sugar
23g Fat (7g sat)	8g Dietary Fiber
16g Protein	32mg Cholesterol
41g Carbohydrates	656mg Sodium

Turkey Cranberry Wrap

Turkey Cranberry Wrap

Makes 2 servings

2 medium whole-wheat tortillas

2 tablespoons chèvre cheese

4 turkey breast slices

¼ cup unsweetened dried cranberries

2 tablespoons chopped pecans

½ cup mixed greens

1 Spread 1 tablespoon of chèvre cheese in the middle of each tortilla.

2 Top with 2 slices of turkey breast, 2 tablespoons dried cranberries, 1 tablespoon chopped pecans, and ¼ cup mixed greens (on each tortilla).

3 Roll up firmly with seam ending on the bottom.

4 Slice in half on the diagonal for serving.

PER SERVING (1 wrap)

275 Calories	1.5g Sugar
9g Fat (2g sat)	5g Dietary Fiber
21g Protein	27mg Cholesterol
27g Carbohydrates	1,011mg Sodium

Grilled Chicken Garden Wrap

Makes 4 servings

1 pound boneless skinless chicken breasts

1 dash each: salt and pepper

1 medium avocado

1 medium red bell pepper, roasted

1 cup arugula or baby spinach

4 (12-inch) whole-wheat tortillas

¼ cup shredded carrots

1 Lightly season the chicken breasts with salt and pepper, and grill or broil until cooked through. Cut into bite-size cubes.

2 Cut the avocado in half, and remove the pit. Scoop out the flesh of the avocado, and slice into thin slices.

3 Slice the red bell pepper into thin strips.

4 To make each wrap, place 1 tortilla on a cutting board, and layer about ½ cup arugula or spinach on top.

5 Add ¼ of the chicken, avocado, and red bell pepper on top of each tortilla. Roll the tortilla up tightly and carefully, with the seam on the side so that it will hold its shape.

6 Cut in half on the diagonal to serve.

PER SERVING (1 wrap)

354 Calories	3.5g Sugar
11g Fat (2g sat)	6g Dietary Fiber
34g Protein	66mg Cholesterol
30g Carbohydrates	253mg Sodium

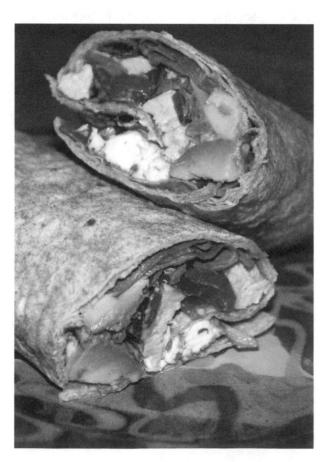

Dr. James Rouse

Spicy Tuna Pita

Makes 2 servings

1 (6-ounce) can tuna in water

½ teaspoon wasabi powder

1 tablespoon diced dill pickle

1 tablespoon diced onion

1 tablespoon diced celery

2 tablespoons low-fat mayonnaise

½ teaspoon mustard

½ teaspoon pepper

4 lettuce leaves

4 slices tomato

2 small whole-wheat pita bread

½ avocado (optional)

1 Drain water from tuna, and add to medium bowl. Add wasabi, pickle, onion, celery, mayonnaise, mustard, and pepper. Stir well to combine.

2 Cut the top ⅓ off from the pita. Open it gently and stuff half the tuna mixture inside. Layer in 2 sliced tomatoes along with 2 pieces of lettuce in each pita.

3 As an option, add 2 thin slices of avocado to each pita.

PER SERVING (1 sandwich)

358 Calories	2.5g Sugar
7g Fat (1g sat)	8g Dietary Fiber
28g Protein	28mg Cholesterol
49g Carbohydrates	771mg Sodium

Avocado Salad Stuffed Pitas

Makes 4 servings

2 avocados

½ medium sweet onion, diced

1 cup chopped tomatoes

½ cup chopped roasted red peppers

½ medium cucumber, peeled, seeded, and chopped

¼ cup chopped fresh cilantro

1 tablespoon lime juice

⅛ teaspoon each: salt and pepper

4 small whole-wheat pita breads

4 leaves red or green leaf lettuce

1 Cut avocados in half, and remove pits. Scoop out with a large spoon, and then chop or dice. Place in bowl.

2 Add onion, tomatoes, red peppers, cucumber, cilantro, lime juice, salt, and pepper, and toss again.

3 Cut top part of pita bread (about ⅓ of the circle). Gently stuff pitas with about ¼ of the avocado salad. Season with salt and pepper to taste.

4 Add 1 red lettuce leaf and enjoy.

PER SERVING (1 sandwich)

366 Calories	4g Sugar
17g Fat (3g sat)	10g Dietary Fiber
10g Protein	0mg Cholesterol
50g Carbohydrates	406mg Sodium

Poultry & Meat

Chicken Marsala

Chicken Marsala

About ⅓ cup flour for dredging (we use brown rice flour, but you can use all-purpose)

4 boneless skinless chicken breasts, pounded thin (1¼ pounds)

2 tablespoons olive oil, divided

1 tablespoon butter

3 cups sliced mushrooms

½ medium red onion, thinly sliced

2 cloves garlic, minced

½ cup dry Marsala wine

1 cup low-sodium chicken or beef broth

1 tablespoon cornstarch

3 tablespoons chopped fresh basil

Salt and pepper to taste

Marsala wine is an Italian fortified wine. You can find Marsala wine at most liquor stores and some grocery stores. We usually use sweet Marsala wine in this recipe.

1. Place flour in a shallow bowl. Pound each chicken breast between 2 sheets of wax paper or plastic wrap. Dredge each chicken breast in the flour, and then pat or shake it so all the excess flour falls off.

2. Heat 1 tablespoon oil plus 1 tablespoon of butter in a large skillet over medium-high heat until hot. Add chicken, and brown about 3 minutes on each side. Transfer to plate, and cover to keep warm.

3. Add remaining tablespoon of olive oil back to the skillet, and return to medium-high heat. Cook mushrooms, onion, and garlic, stirring often for 3–4 minutes.

4. Add the Marsala wine, and simmer for another 3 minutes.

5. Combine broth and cornstarch; mix well. Add broth mixture to skillet, and return chicken to skillet. Simmer uncovered 2–3 minutes or until sauce thickens, stirring occasionally.

6. Serve each chicken breast topped with ¼ mushroom mixture over whole-grain noodles or brown rice. Top with fresh basil, and season with salt and pepper, if desired.

PER SERVING

300 Calories	<1g Sugar
12g Fat (3g sat)	1g Dietary Fiber
37g Protein	90mg Cholesterol
7g Carbohydrates	136mg Sodium

Sautéed Chicken with Olives and Tomatoes

Makes 4 servings

1 pound boneless, skinless chicken breasts, chopped

1 tablespoon olive oil

½ medium onion, chopped

2 cups diced fire roasted tomatoes

½ cup chopped kalamata olives

1 garlic clove, minced

¼ teaspoon oregano

¼ cup chopped fresh basil

Salt and pepper to taste

1 Slice or chop chicken breast into bite-size pieces. Set aside.

2 Add olive oil to a deep-sided skillet, and heat over medium high. Add onion, and stir for about 4 minutes.

3 Add chicken to pan, stir, and cook another 5 minutes until chicken starts to brown.

4 Add tomatoes, olives, garlic, and oregano. Stir again, and cook for another 5 minutes over low heat.

5 Stir in fresh basil, and season with salt and pepper to taste.

PER SERVING

241 Calories	4g Sugar
13g Fat (1g sat)	trace Dietary Fiber
26g Protein	66mg Cholesterol
4g Carbohydrates	546mg Sodium

Dr. James Rouse

Enchiladas

Makes 6 servings

2 tablespoons safflower or grapeseed oil

1 pound ground turkey (or use lean ground beef or buffalo)

1 onion, minced

1 clove garlic, minced

8 ounces diced green chiles

1 cup diced tomatoes

½ teaspoon salt

½ teaspoon pepper

½ teaspoon ground cumin

½ teaspoon chili powder

2 tablespoons cooking oil

2 cups grated low-fat Cheddar cheese

12 small corn or flour tortillas

2 cups enchilada sauce

To cut calories, fat, and sodium, reduce total cheese to one cup and leave cheese out of the inside of the enchiladas.

1 In a large skillet, heat oil and ground turkey, and cook until almost done, breaking up the ground turkey into crumbles.

2 Add onion, and sauté until almost tender. Add garlic, green chilies, tomatoes, salt, pepper, cumin, and chili powder, and stir. Simmer uncovered for about 10 minutes.

3 In another skillet with deep sides, add 2 tablespoons of cooking oil, and fry tortillas 15–20 seconds each side; remove to a large baking tray layered with paper towels, or a kitchen towel, to absorb excess oil.

4 Fill each tortilla with about 2 tablespoons turkey mixture and 2 teaspoons of shredded cheese. Roll, and place in greased shallow baking dish.

5 Pour enchilada sauce over enchiladas, top with remaining grated cheese, and bake uncovered at 350° for 15 minutes.

PER SERVING

698 Calories	1.5g Sugar
34g Fat (10g sat)	5g Dietary Fiber
33g Protein	92mg Cholesterol
65g Carbohydrates	1090mg Sodium

POULTRY & MEAT

Stuffed Chicken Breasts

Stuffed Chicken Breasts

Makes 4 servings

4 boneless skinless chicken breast halves (about 1 pound), pounded ½ inch thick

⅛ teaspoon salt

⅛ teaspoon ground black pepper

2 tablespoons olive oil, divided

1 tablespoon unsalted butter

1 cup thinly sliced mushrooms

1 small sweet onion, thinly sliced

3 cups spinach leaves

2 ounces feta cheese

If a sauce is desired, deglaze the skillet with 4 tablespoons white wine. Simmer for a few minutes, then return chicken to skillet. Serve warm, and drizzle sauce over top of chicken.

1 Season chicken breasts with salt and pepper. Slice through each chicken breast horizontally without cutting through it; leave intact about ¼ inch from the opposite side. Spread open, and gently pound again.

2 Heat 1 tablespoon oil in a large skillet over moderate heat. Add butter, mushrooms, and onion. Sauté for about 5 minutes.

3 Stir in spinach leaves, and cook until spinach has wilted considerably. Stir in feta cheese, and place mixture in a bowl.

4 Spoon 1–2 tablespoons of the mixture into the center of the chicken breasts. Fold, and press well to seal. (You can use a toothpick to secure.)

5 Return the skillet to the stove over medium-high heat. Add remaining tablespoon of olive oil, and swirl around so that the skillet is well coated.

6 Add stuffed breasts to the pan, and brown on both sides, cooking 10–12 minutes total.

PER SERVING

252 Calories	<1g Sugar
11g Fat (5g sat)	1g Dietary Fiber
31g Protein	89mg Cholesterol
5g Carbohydrates	322mg Sodium

Mexican Meatloaf

Makes 8 servings

1 tablespoon olive oil

½ cup chopped red onion

1 celery rib, finely chopped

1 garlic clove, minced

1 pound ground buffalo

6 ounces chorizo

1 large egg, lightly beaten

½ teaspoon salt

½ teaspoon black pepper

½ teaspoon ground cumin

½ cup rolled oats

½ cup ketchup, divided

1 chipotle chile canned in adobo sauce, chopped

1 teaspoon brown sugar

1 medium tomato, seeded and chopped

1 Preheat the oven to 375°. Prepare 5x9-inch loaf pan by coating lightly with cooking oil spray.

2 Heat olive oil in a large skillet over medium-high heat. Add onion, celery, and garlic, and stir for about 5 minutes. Set aside for a few minutes to cool.

3 In a large bowl, combine ground buffalo, chorizo, egg, salt, pepper, cumin, oats, and ¼ cup ketchup. Mix thoroughly. Add onion mixture, and mix again.

4 Place the meat mixture into prepared loaf pan.

5 In the bowl of a food processor, combine remaining ¼ cup ketchup, chipotle chile, brown sugar, and tomato. Purée until smooth. Spread this saucy mixture on top of meatloaf.

6 Bake for 40–45 minutes until meat is cooked through. Pour off excess juices.

PER SERVING

296 Calories	5g Sugar
19g Fat (4g sat)	1g Dietary Fiber
20g Protein	91mg Cholesterol
10g Carbohydrates	640mg Sodium

Dr. James Rouse

Beef and Broccoli

Makes 5 servings

Water chestnuts actually grow underwater and can be eaten raw, grilled, pickled, or boiled. You can find them canned at most grocery stores; fresh water chestnuts can be found in Asian markets. They are a good source of fiber and are naturally low in fat.

2 tablespoons minced garlic

1 tablespoon grated fresh ginger

2 teaspoons mirin*

2 tablespoons low-sodium soy sauce

2 teaspoons teriyaki sauce

2 tablespoons low-sodium beef broth

2 teaspoons honey

1 tablespoon sesame oil

2 tablespoons canola oil

1 pound steak, thinly sliced across the grain

1 pound broccoli, cut into florets (about 5 cups)

¼ cup water chestnuts

¼ cup chopped green onions

½ teaspoon red pepper flakes

1¼ cups cooked brown rice, for serving

2 tablespoons chopped fresh mint

1 Combine the garlic, ginger, mirin, soy sauce, teriyaki sauce, broth, and honey in a small mixing bowl. Mix well, and set aside until ready to use.

2 Heat a wok or a large skillet over medium high. Add sesame and canola oils and sliced beef, stirring frequently until meat is just starting to brown.

3 Reduce heat to medium, and add broccoli, water chestnuts, and green onions. Cook for 2–3 minutes.

4 Slowly and carefully pour sauce over meat and broccoli mixture. Lower heat, cover, and cook for about 3 minutes.

5 Stir in red pepper flakes. Cover again, and cook for 1–2 more minutes.

6 Serve immediately over brown rice, and sprinkle with fresh mint.

*Mirin is a sweet rice wine used in Japanese cooking (sometimes confused with rice wine vinegar). It doesn't just flavor food, it gives luster to sauces and glazes and can help them cling to food.

PER SERVING

375 Calories	4.3g Sugar
25g Fat (7g sat)	3g Dietary Fiber
17g Protein	51mg Cholesterol
22g Carbohydrates	403mg Sodium

Marinated Steak with Pomegranate Sauce

Makes 4 servings

1½ pounds flank steak or tenderloin

⅓ cup low-sodium soy sauce

⅓ cup red wine vinegar

2 tablespoons honey

2 tablespoons grated gingerroot

1 garlic clove, minced

½ teaspoon ground cinnamon

1 small onion, sliced

POMEGRANATE SAUCE:

6 fluid ounces 100% pomegranate juice (no sugar added)

¼ cup low-sodium beef broth

1 sprig thyme

1 small cinnamon stick

2 tablespoons red wine, such as Pinot Noir

½ cup pomegranate seeds (arils)

1 Place meat in a large shallow glass baking dish. Combine soy sauce, vinegar, honey, ginger, garlic, and cinnamon, and pour over meat. Place sliced onion on top of meat. Cover, and marinate for at least 2 hours and up to 24 hours. Turn once while marinating. While steak is marinating, prepare Sauce.

2 Combine pomegranate juice, broth, thyme sprig, and cinnamon stick in a saucepan, and bring to a boil, then reduce heat to low and simmer for 20–30 minutes or until reduced by half. Remove thyme sprig and cinnamon stick. Stir in the red wine, and remove from heat. If a thick Sauce is desired, you can add a little bit (½ teaspoon) of cornstarch.

3 Bring steak to room temperature. Preheat grill to medium high, or preheat broiler. Grill 5–7 minutes on each side for medium-rare.

4 Allow steak to rest 5–8 minutes before slicing. Slice thinly on the diagonal across grain of the meat.

5 Serve steak drizzled with 2 tablespoons of Sauce and 1 teaspoon pomegranate seeds.

NOTE: An Israeli study suggests that pomegranate juice may offer health benefits for diabetics, despite the juice containing significant sugar concentrations. "PJ consumption by diabetic patients did not worsen the diabetic parameters, but rather resulted in anti-oxidative effects on serum and macrophages, which could contribute to attenuation of atherosclerosis development in these patients." [Atherosclerosis. 2006 Aug;187(2):363-71.]

PER SERVING

411 Calories	17g Sugar
18g Fat (0g sat)	3g Dietary Fiber
36g Protein	87mg Cholesterol
26g Carbohydrates	929mg Sodium

Dr. James Rouse

Lamb Kebabs

Makes 6 servings

½ cup diced onions

1 medium garlic clove, chopped

2 ounces red wine vinegar (¼ cup)

1 teaspoon salt

½ teaspoon black pepper

1 teaspoon chopped fresh oregano

2 tablespoons olive oil

1 teaspoon ground cumin

2 teaspoons ground coriander

½ teaspoon ground cinnamon

2 pounds boneless lamb shoulder, cut in 2-inch cubes

2 medium red bell peppers, seeded and cut into 1-inch pieces

1 teaspoon chopped fresh mint

1 Combine the first 10 ingredients in a large nonmetal bowl. Add the lamb. Cover, and marinate for 2 hours.

2 Soak 12 skewers in water while the lamb is marinating.

3 Place 3–4 cubes of lamb on each of the skewers, alternating with red bell pepper pieces.

4 Grill or broil to desired doneness. Garnish with fresh mint.

PER SERVING

335 Calories	0g Sugar
25g Fat (9g sat)	1g Dietary Fiber
22g Protein	82mg Cholesterol
5g Carbohydrates	424mg Sodium

Sesame Pork

Sesame Pork

Makes 4 servings

1¼ pounds boneless pork chops

1 teaspoon minced fresh ginger

2 tablespoons low-sodium tamari soy sauce

1 small scallion, well rinsed and finely chopped

2 tablespoons rice vinegar

1 tablespoon honey or agave nectar

1 teaspoon sesame oil, divided

2 tablespoons sesame seeds

1 teaspoon olive oil

1. Pound and flatten pork loin chops into about ¼-inch thickness.

2. Whisk together ginger, tamari, scallion, rice vinegar, honey, and ½ teaspoon sesame oil.

3. Add pork chops, and marinate for 30 minutes to a few hours, covered, in the refrigerator.

4. Remove from marinade. Press sesame seeds into pork chops. Heat remaining sesame oil and olive oil in nonstick pan over medium heat. Add chops, and brown, cooking on both sides for 4–5 minutes or until pork is cooked through.

5. Add marinade to pan, and bring to a low simmer. Lower heat, and cook another few minutes, until pork is cooked through.

NOTE: This dish can also be made more like a typical stir-fry by slicing the pork into bite-size pieces, stir-frying it in the oils, and adding the marinade sauce (minus the sesame seeds) halfway through the cooking. Sprinkle the sesame seeds over the entire dish when serving.

PER SERVING

363 Calories	4g Sugar
18g Fat (5g sat)	1g Dietary Fiber
38g Protein	111mg Cholesterol
10g Carbohydrates	369mg Sodium

POULTRY & MEAT

Chipotle Pork Tenderloin

1 medium chipotle chile canned in adobo sauce

1 tablespoon chopped shallots

1 tablespoon adobo sauce

1½ pounds pork tenderloin

¼ cup plain nonfat Greek-style yogurt

1 teaspoon prepared mustard

½ teaspoon salt

½ teaspoon pepper

½ teaspoon cumin powder

1 teaspoon brown sugar

⅛ teaspoon cayenne pepper

SAUCE:

1 chipotle chile canned in adobo sauce

2 tablespoons pure maple syrup

3 tablespoons low-sodium chicken broth

1 tablespoon apple cider vinegar

3 tablespoons plain nonfat Greek-style yogurt

To reduce total amount of sugar, make the Sauce without the maple syrup. If you like the maple flavor, you can add maple extract and a ¼ teaspoon of Stevia.

1 Preheat grill to medium high.

2 Combine chile, shallots, and adobo sauce in small bowl. Set aside.

3 Trim the silverskin from the pork tenderloin. (This is the tough whitish membrane on top of the meat.) Slice the tenderloin horizontally about ⅔ of the way through; this should leave about ¼–½ inch from the other side.

4 Open the tenderloin, and spread chipotle mixture down the center. Fold back together, pressing to adhere.

5 Combine yogurt, mustard, salt, pepper, cumin, brown sugar, and cayenne in a small mixing bowl. Brush the mixture onto the pork tenderloin, covering all sides.

6 Brush the grill with vegetable oil. Place the pork on the grill, cover, and cook for 12–15 minutes, turning every few minutes for even cooking. Continue to brush the yogurt mixture over the pork while it is cooking. When the pork reaches an internal temperature of about 150°, remove it from the grill, and allow to rest for 10 minutes.

7 Combine Sauce ingredients. Slice tenderloin, and top with Sauce.

PER SERVING

289 Calories	18g Sugar
8g Fat (3g sat)	1g Dietary Fiber
40g Protein	113mg Cholesterol
11g Carbohydrates	500mg Sodium

Fennel-Crusted Pork Loin with Swiss Chard

Makes 6 servings

1 tablespoon fennel seeds, crushed

1 teaspoon salt

1 teaspoon pepper

2 pounds lean, boneless pork loin

1 small red onion

1 medium fennel bulb, trimmed from the top and thinly sliced

1 tablespoon olive oil

1 teaspoon unsalted butter

2 garlic cloves, minced

¼ cup white wine (Sauvignon Blanc or Pinot Grigio)

½ cup low-sodium chicken broth

½ teaspoon fresh lemon juice, or to taste

1 bunch Swiss chard, or spinach, chopped

Crush fennel seeds with a mortar and pestle, or place in a plastic baggie, and crush with a mallet or rolling pin.

1 Preheat oven to 450° with rack in middle.

2 Combine crushed fennel seeds with salt and pepper to make a rub.

3 Place the pork on a rack in a roasting pan. Pat dry, then with clean hands, press the rub onto the pork.

4 Roast the pork for about 30 minutes. Reduce heat to 400° and roast for another 45 minutes to an hour. Once the internal temperature has reached 155°, remove pork from the oven, and allow to rest about 15 minutes before slicing.

5 Meanwhile, slice onion and fennel. While pork is resting, heat a large skillet on medium high, and add olive oil, butter, onion, and fennel. Reduce heat to medium; cook and stir about 5 minutes.

6 Add garlic, wine, and chicken broth, and simmer for a few more minutes. Stir in lemon juice and chard, and cook for about 3 minutes, stirring frequently until chard has completely wilted.

7 Slice pork loin into ¼-inch thick slices.

8 To serve, spoon chard mixture onto plate, and top with a few slices of pork.

PER SERVING

240 Calories	0g Sugar
10g Fat (3g sat)	2g Dietary Fiber
29g Protein	70mg Cholesterol
7g Carbohydrates	484mg Sodium

Slow Cooked Pork

Makes 6 servings

2 pounds boneless pork loin

2 large red bell peppers, seeded and cut into strips

1 medium yellow sweet onion, thinly sliced

½ cup low-sodium teriyaki sauce

¼ cup water

2 tablespoons rice wine vinegar

1 tablespoon red pepper flakes

1 tablespoon minced fresh ginger

1 tablespoon minced garlic

¼ cup almond butter

½ cup lite coconut milk

2 limes for garnish

Alternatively, enjoy on a hoagie roll topped with a bit of broccoli slaw . . . delicious! (See page 139.)

1 Coat slow cooker with nonstick cooking spray. Put the pork, bell peppers, onion, teriyaki sauce, water, rice vinegar, red pepper flakes, ginger, and garlic in the cooker. Cover, and cook on LOW until the pork is fork-tender, 6–8 hours. (Periodically check the slow cooker to make sure the liquid has not completely been absorbed. If all signs of liquid are gone, add a little more water and a little more teriyaki, and loosen any browned bits on the bottom. You could also add low-sodium chicken broth.)

2 Remove the pork from the cooker, and coarsely chop or shred.

3 Add the almond butter to the liquid in the cooker, and stir with a whisk until well blended.

4   Whisk in coconut milk. Return the shredded pork to the sauce, and toss to coat the meat evenly.

5 Serve over hot brown rice. Garnish with lime wedges.

PER SERVING

257 Calories	3.5g Sugar
13g Fat (4g sat)	2g Dietary Fiber
23g Protein	47mg Cholesterol
14g Carbohydrates	967mg Sodium

Seafood

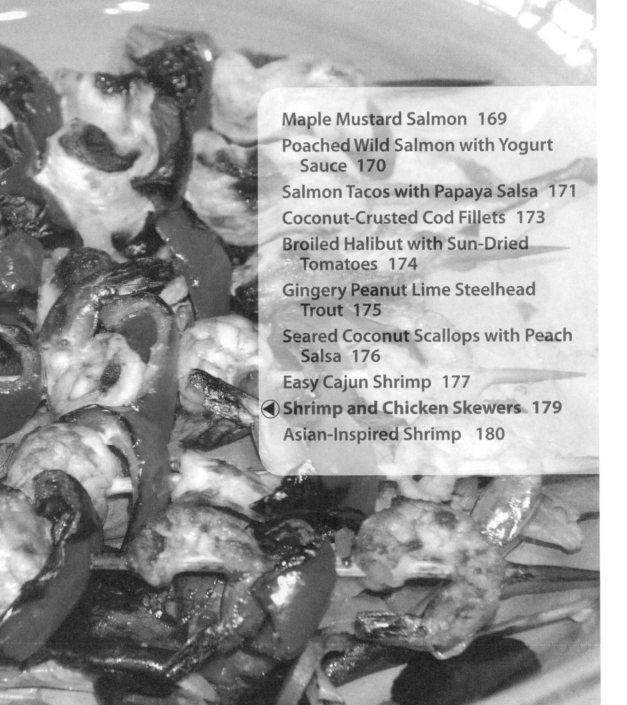

Maple Mustard Salmon

Maple Mustard Salmon

1 tablespoon Dijon mustard

1 tablespoon maple syrup

1 teaspoon red wine vinegar

¼ teaspoon salt

⅛ teaspoon freshly ground black pepper

20 ounces wild salmon fillets

1 Preheat oven to 475°.

2 Mix together mustard, maple syrup, vinegar, salt, and pepper. Brush generous layer onto the top of salmon fillets.

3 Place salmon on a baking pan or broiler pan lined with foil, and cook for 12–15 minutes, until the fish flakes easily when tested with a fork.

4 Serve warm or at room temperature.

PER SERVING

264 Calories	2g Sugar
11g Fat (2g sat)	trace Dietary Fiber
35g Protein	96mg Cholesterol
4g Carbohydrates	257mg Sodium

Poached Wild Salmon with Yogurt Sauce

Makes 4 servings

1 cup water

½ cup dry white wine

1 small onion, sliced

2 sprigs dill

3 peppercorns

¼ teaspoon salt

4 wild salmon fillets (4–5 ounces each)

YOGURT SAUCE:

½ cup plain nonfat Greek-style yogurt

¼ cup seeded and finely chopped cucumber

1 tablespoon minced sweet onion

¼ teaspoon salt

½ teaspoon chopped fresh dill

1 tablespoon fresh lemon juice

1 In a large, deep-sided skillet, combine all ingredients except salmon fillets. Place skillet over medium-high heat, and cook until mixture starts to boil. Lower heat, and place salmon fillets on top. Cover, and cook for about 7 minutes, or until salmon barely flakes when tested with a fork.

2 Carefully remove salmon from liquid, and place on serving plate. Serve hot or cold. To serve cold, refrigerate until ready to serve. Serve with Yogurt Sauce.

3 To prepare Yogurt Sauce, combine yogurt, cucumber, onion, salt, dill, and lemon juice; mix well.

PER SERVING

191 Calories	3g Sugar
5g Fat (1g sat)	1.1g Dietary Fiber
26g Protein	62mg Cholesterol
6g Carbohydrates	367mg Sodium

Dr. James Rouse

Salmon Tacos with Papaya Salsa

Makes 4 servings

2 tablespoons fresh lime juice

1 tablespoon olive oil

1 garlic clove, minced

1¼ teaspoons dried oregano

1⅜ teaspoons sea salt

1⅜ teaspoons black pepper

1 pound salmon fillet

PAPAYA SALSA:

1 avocado, peeled, pitted, and chopped

1 papaya, peeled, seeded, and diced

1 tablespoon chopped fresh cilantro

1 cup cherry tomatoes, halved

2 tablespoons lime juice

1 jalapeño chile pepper, seeded and diced

TACOS:

8 (6½-inch) corn tortillas, warmed

2 cups shredded cabbage or lettuce

1 Whisk together the first 6 ingredients.

2 Rinse salmon, pat dry, and place it in a shallow dish for marinating. Pour the lime marinade over salmon, cover, and let marinate for 30–60 minutes in the refrigerator.

3 Meanwhile, prepare Papaya Salsa by mixing all salsa ingredients together in a nonmetal bowl.

4 Heat grill to medium high. Grill salmon for about 5 minutes on each side or until just barely opaque all the way through. Remove from heat, allow to rest about 3 minutes, and then flake salmon into large pieces.

5 Place 2 warmed tortillas on each plate. Place even portions of salmon in each tortilla (about 2 ounces each). Top each taco with cabbage or lettuce and 1–2 tablespoons of Papaya Salsa, portioned evenly. Fold tortillas over, and serve with additional chopped cilantro, if desired.

PER SERVING

405 Calories	4.5g Sugar
17g Fat (3g sat)	6g Dietary Fiber
27g Protein	59mg Cholesterol
40g Carbohydrates	825mg Sodium

Coconut-Crusted Cod Fillets

Coconut-Crusted Cod Fillets

Makes 4 servings

¾ cup rice flour for dredging, divided

1 medium egg

1 tablespoon water

½ cup unsweetened coconut meat, shredded

½ teaspoon salt

¼ teaspoon pepper

1 pound cod fillets

1 tablespoon butter

1 tablespoon olive oil

TROPICAL SALSA:

2 ripe peaches (medium size), pitted, peeled, and chopped

½ cup skinned, seeded, and diced papaya

1 medium yellow tomato, diced

½ medium red bell pepper, seeded and diced

¼ cup chopped green onions

2 tablespoons fresh lime juice

1 teaspoon minced fresh ginger

2 tablespoons chopped fresh cilantro

1 tablespoon chopped fresh mint

1 Set out 3 shallow bowls for dredging. In first bowl, add ½ cup rice flour. In second bowl, whisk egg with water. In third bowl, mix together the shredded coconut, remaining ¼ cup rice flour, salt, and pepper.

2 Dredge each fillet first in plain flour (shaking off excess), then brush or dip with egg/water mixture, and then dredge in coconut mixture, pressing the coconut to the fish to make sure it sticks. Set on plate as each fillet is coated.

3 Heat butter and oil in a skillet over medium-high heat. Add fillets, and cook on each side until lightly browned and cooked through the middle, roughly 3–4 minutes each side, depending on thickness of fillet.

4 Combine all Tropical Salsa ingredients in a medium bowl, and toss to mix well. Cover, and refrigerate for at least 30 minutes before serving.

PER SERVING (1 fillet)

342 Calories	2g Sugar
15g Fat (9g sat)	2g Dietary Fiber
24g Protein	110mg Cholesterol
26g Carbohydrates	378mg Sodium

PER SERVING (⅓ cup salsa)

52 Calories	9g Sugar
trace Fat	3g Dietary Fiber
1g Protein	0mg Cholesterol
13g Carbohydrates	15mg Sodium

Broiled Halibut with Sun-Dried Tomatoes

Makes 4 servings

1 pound halibut fillets, about ¾ inch thick

8 sun-dried tomato halves

1 tablespoon diced red onion

2 tablespoons chopped fresh parsley

⅛ teaspoon salt

⅛ teaspoon freshly ground pepper

2 tablespoons olive oil

1 Preheat broiler. Spray a thin coat of olive oil cooking spray on the broiler pan, or line the pan with foil or parchment.

2 Place the halibut on the rack in the broiler pan. Place on the top oven shelf, about 4 inches from the heat. Broil for about 7 minutes.

3 If you are using non oil-packed sun-dried tomatoes, place them in 1 cup of hot water. Soak for about 5 minutes or until soft. Drain and finely chop.

4 Mix together tomatoes, diced red onion, parsley, salt, pepper, and olive oil. Spread over the top of the fish.

5 Broil approximately 2–3 minutes longer or until the fish flakes with a fork.

PER SERVING

202 Calories	1.2g Sugar
10g Fat (1g sat)	1g Dietary Fiber
25g Protein	36mg Cholesterol
4g Carbohydrates	255mg Sodium

Dr. James Rouse

Gingery Peanut Lime Steelhead Trout

Makes 4 servings

Steelhead Trout is a delicious alternative to salmon. It actually looks and tastes like salmon, eats the same diet as salmon (krill), swims up river to spawn, and is a great source of omega-3 fatty acids, which are naturally anti-inflammatory. Yet, it is a type of rainbow trout. You can substitute steelhead trout in any recipe calling for salmon.

4 (5-ounce) steelhead trout (or salmon) fillets, skin removed

1 (14-ounce) can lite coconut milk

1 tablespoon peanut butter

2 tablespoons lime juice

2 inches fresh ginger, peeled and chopped

2 garlic cloves, finely chopped

1 teaspoon ground coriander

1 pinch sea salt, or to taste

2 cups cooked brown jasmine rice

4 cups chopped broccoli, steamed

2 tablespoons chopped fresh basil

1 Preheat oven to 400°.

2 Place the fish fillets in a shallow ovenproof baking dish.

3 Whisk together the coconut milk, peanut butter, lime juice, ginger, garlic, coriander, and salt. Pour this mixture on top of the fish. Bake for 25–35 minutes or until desired doneness.

4 Serve fish on a bed of cooked brown jasmine rice with a side of steamed broccoli. Serve with fresh chopped basil on top.

PER SERVING
(includes rice and broccoli)

332 Calories	<1g Sugar
8g Fat (1g sat)	4g Dietary Fiber
34g Protein	74mg Cholesterol
31g Carbohydrates	136mg Sodium

Seared Coconut Scallops with Peach Salsa

Makes 5 servings

1½ pounds large scallops

1 cup lite coconut milk

Salt and pepper to taste

1 tablespoon butter

1 tablespoon olive oil

PEACH SALSA:

3 medium peaches, peeled and chopped

¼ cup skinned, seeded, and diced papaya

1 medium yellow tomato, diced

½ medium red bell pepper, seeded and diced

¼ cup chopped green onions

2 tablespoons fresh lime juice

1 teaspoon minced fresh ginger

2 tablespoons chopped fresh cilantro

1 tablespoon chopped fresh mint

OPTIONAL GARNISHES:

Toasted shredded, unsweetened coconut meat

Chopped macadamia nuts

Additional mint and cilantro

1 Rinse scallops to remove grit, and place in a bowl with coconut milk. Cover, and refrigerate for about an hour.

2 Meanwhile, combine Peach Salsa ingredients in a medium bowl, and toss gently to mix. Cover and refrigerate.

3 Cover a large plate with paper towels. Remove the scallops one at a time from the coconut milk and place on the towel. Pat dry on top. Season tops of scallops with a small amount of salt and pepper.

4 Heat a large skillet over medium high heat. Add butter and olive oil, and stir together until butter is melted and skillet is hot. Add scallops one at a time to the skillet; salt and pepper sides down. Let the bottoms of the scallops acquire a nice brown sear (this takes 3–4 minutes on each side). Use tongs or a small spatula to flip scallops.

5 Transfer scallops to serving plates, and top with a few tablespoons of salsa. Garnish with a sprinkle of shredded coconut, macadamia nuts, chopped mint, and cilantro.

PER SERVING

180 Calories	7g Sugar
4g Fat (2g sat)	2g Dietary Fiber
24g Protein	45mg Cholesterol
13g Carbohydrates	243mg Sodium

Easy Cajun Shrimp

Makes 4 servings

1¼ pounds shrimp, peeled and deveined

1 teaspoon paprika

¾ teaspoon thyme

¾ teaspoon dried oregano

½ teaspoon garlic powder

¼ teaspoon sea salt

⅛ teaspoon black pepper

1 teaspoon chili sauce

1 tablespoon olive oil

1 Combine all ingredients except olive oil into a large plastic zipper bag. Seal the bag, and shake until shrimp is well coated.

2 Heat oil in a large skillet or wok over medium high. Add shrimp mixture, and stir-fry about 4 minutes or until shrimp are cooked.

3 Serve over a bed of greens or brown basmati rice.

PER SERVING

185 Calories	0 Sugar
6g Fat (1g sat)	trace Dietary Fiber
29g Protein	216mg Cholesterol
2g Carbohydrates	328mg Sodium

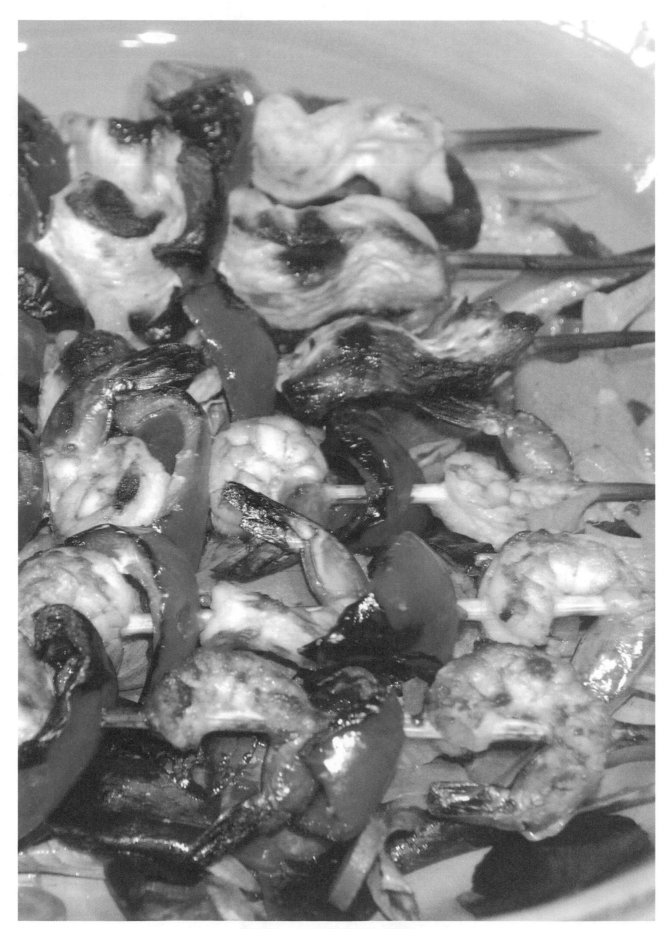

Shrimp and Chicken Skewers

Shrimp and Chicken Skewers

Makes 4 servings

Serve with a large mixed green salad topped with your favorite vinaigrette.

¼ cup lemon juice

1 garlic clove, minced

1 tablespoon red wine vinegar

1 tablespoon lemon zest

⅓ cup olive oil

⅛ teaspoon salt

⅛ teaspoon pepper

16 medium shrimp

2 red bell peppers, seeded and cut into large bite-size pieces

¾ pound boneless skinless chicken breasts, cut into thin strips

1 Whisk together first 7 ingredients.

2 Peel, devein, rinse, and dry shrimp. Thread shrimp onto a long metal skewer (4 shrimp per skewer), alternating with red bell pepper pieces.

3 Do the same with the pieces of chicken, alternating with red bell pepper in between each strip of chicken.

4 Brush each skewer with marinade, and pour remaining marinade on top of skewers.

5 Heat grill over medium high. Grill chicken for about 5 minutes per side, or until cooked through, and grill shrimp for about 4 minutes per side.

If you prefer to use wooden skewers, soak them in water about 1 hour, then drain prior to threading. This should prevent the skewers from burning.

PER SERVING

291 Calories	1.5g Sugar
19g Fat (3g sat)	1g Dietary Fiber
25g Protein	92mg Cholesterol
4g Carbohydrates	172mg Sodium

Asian-Inspired Shrimp

Makes 6 servings

1 tablespoon peanut or canola oil

½ cup thinly sliced onion

2 teaspoons red curry paste

1 tablespoon peeled and minced ginger

¼ cup lite coconut milk

1 tablespoon lime juice

¼ cup low-sodium chicken broth

1 teaspoon low-sodium soy sauce

1½ pounds raw medium shrimp, peeled and deveined

¼ cup chopped fresh cilantro

Salt and pepper to taste

1 Heat oil in a large skillet over medium-high heat. Add onion, and stir for about 2 minutes.

2 Add curry paste and ginger, and continue to stir for 2–3 more minutes.

3 Add coconut milk, lime juice, broth, and soy sauce. Allow mixture to come to a low boil, and simmer for 2 minutes.

4 Add shrimp, and cook until just opaque in center, stirring often, for about 4 minutes.

5 Add cilantro, reduce heat to low, continue to stir for another minute, and then turn off heat. Season to taste.

Tastes great over noodles or jasmine brown rice.

PER SERVING

192 Calories	0g Sugar
2g Fat	6g Dietary Fiber
21g Protein	115mg Cholesterol
22g Carbohydrates	382mg Sodium

Dr. James Rouse

Desserts

Carrot Zucchini Cake with Whipped Cream Frosting

Carrot Zucchini Cake
with Whipped Cream Frosting

Makes 12 servings

CAKE:

½ cup canola oil

½ cup brown sugar

4 eggs

2 cups whole-wheat pastry flour

2 teaspoons cinnamon

½ teaspoon ground ginger

¼ teaspoon allspice

1 tablespoon Stevia

2 teaspoons baking soda

1 cup finely shredded carrots

1 cup finely shredded zucchini, drained of excess moisture

WHIPPED CREAM FROSTING:

4 ounces Neufchâtel cream cheese, softened

¼ cup powdered sugar

1 tablespoon vanilla extract

1 cup heavy whipping cream

2 tablespoons finely chopped walnuts (optional)

PER SERVING (1 slice)

323 Calories	13g Sugar
21g Fat (7g sat)	3g Dietary Fiber
6g Protein	105mg Cholesterol
29g Carbohydrates	287mg Sodium

1 Preheat oven to 350°. Prepare 2 (8- or 9-inch) round cake pans by coating lighlty with cooking oil spray,

2 Cream together oil and brown sugar in a large bowl, using electric mixer. Add eggs, one at a time, beating between additions.

3 In a separate bowl, whisk together flour, cinnamon, ginger, allspice, Stevia, and baking soda.

4 Stir dry mixture into wet ingredients. Fold in carrots and zucchini.

5 Pour batter evenly into the 2 pans. Bake 30–35 minutes. Cool on racks for at least 10 minutes before removing from pans.

6 Using electric mixer, prepare Whipped Cream Frosting by whipping together the cream cheese, sugar, and vanilla. While whipping, slowly pour in the whipping cream. Scrape the bottom of the bowl a few times while you continue whipping and the mixture starts to stiffen.

7 Frost the top of one cake layer with ⅓–½ cup of frosting. Place the other layer on top, and frost top and side. Sprinkle chopped walnuts on top, if desired. Cover, and keep refrigerated.

8 To serve, cut into 12 wedges.

Apple Oat Crisp

Makes 10 servings

While fruit sugar can raise blood glucose rapidly, other substances in fruit, such as fibers and pectin, may have a protective and positive affect in individuals with diabetes. It is very important to distinguish between whole fruits and fruit juices because with fruit juices, you are getting a much higher dose of sugars.

1 (9-inch) prepared (or homemade) pie crust

9 apples, cored, peeled, and sliced

1½ teaspoons cinnamon, divided

Juice from ½ lemon

⅓ cup brown sugar, divided

1 teaspoon cornstarch

1 cup rolled oats

¼ cup finely chopped walnuts

½ cup brown rice flour

2 tablespoons melted unsalted butter

1 Preheat oven to 375°. Spray pie dish with cooking oil spray, and line with crust.

2 Place sliced apples in large bowl. Stir in ½ teaspoon cinnamon, lemon juice, 2 tablespoons brown sugar, and cornstarch. Mix well. Spread into bottom of prepared pie dish.

3 Stir together remaining brown sugar, remaining cinnamon, oats, walnuts, and flour, and pulse in food processor until walnuts are well chopped.

4 Add melted butter, and stir until the mixture is well combined and crumbly. Distribute topping evenly on top.

5 Bake 45 minutes or until top is lightly browned and apples have softened.

6 To serve, cut into 10 wedges.

CRUSTLESS VARIATION:

Omit the pie crust and prepare in the same manner.

PER SERVING without pie crust

188 Calories	14g Sugar
5g Fat (2g sat)	5g Dietary Fiber
3g Protein	6mg Cholesterol
35g Carbohydrates	3mg Sodium

PER SERVING (1 slice)

268 Calories	14g Sugar
10g Fat (3g sat)	5g Dietary Fiber
4g Protein	6mg Cholesterol
43g Carbohydrates	119mg Sodium

Cashew Chocolate Frosting

Makes 1⅛ cups (12 servings)

1½ cups cashews, soaked in pure water for 4 hours

½ cup warm water

2 dates

¼ cup bittersweet chocolate chips

½ teaspoon vanilla extract

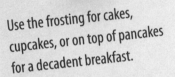

Use the frosting for cakes, cupcakes, or on top of pancakes for a decadent breakfast.

1 Soak cashews in pure water to cover for about 4 hours.

2 In separate bowl, combine ½ cup warm water and dates. Soak dates for 30 minutes. Remove, and save soaking water. Remove pits from dates.

3 Blend/purée soaked cashews in blender or food processor.

4 Add pitted dates, and blend again; add water by the tablespoon, as needed to help achieve a smooth consistency.

5 Melt chocolate chips using double boiler method or in a nonmetallic bowl in the microwave, first for 30 seconds, then stirring, and then 15 more seconds. That is all it should take to melt the chips completely. Stir melted chocolate into cashew mixture. Pulse to thoroughly blend in the chocolate.

PER SERVING (1½ tablespoons)

115 Calories	5g Sugar
9g Fat (2g sat)	1g Dietary Fiber
3g Protein	0mg Cholesterol
8g Carbohydrates	3mg Sodium

Beet Cupcakes

Beet Cupcakes

Makes 12 servings

Beets add natural sweetness, fiber, and gorgeous color to these healthy treats. Sugar is much lower than in a typical cupcake. We like to serve with whipped cream frosting, our healthy version of a red velvet cupcake.

3 whole beets

¼ cup Greek-style yogurt

2 ounces bittersweet chocolate chips, melted

1¼ cups oat flour

1 teaspoon baking soda

¼ teaspoon salt

¼ cup unsalted butter, softened

⅓ cup sugar

1 tablespoon Stevia

1 teaspoon vanilla extract

1 medium egg, beaten

May sprinkle lightly with powdered sugar, or frost with Whipped Cream Frosting (page 183) or Cashew Chocolate Frosting (page 185), if desired. Of course, this alters the nutrional values.

1 Heat oven to 400°. Wash and dry beets, and place on baking sheet. Roast about 35 minutes, or until they start to soften. Remove from oven, and allow to cool.

2 Reduce oven temperature to 350°. Line a 12-cup muffin tin with paper liners.

3 When beets have cooled, peel, and discard outer skin. Chop, and add to bowl of food processor. Add yogurt, and purée until smooth.

4 Melt chocolate using a double boiler, or in a microwave-safe bowl, stirring in 30-second increments until melted.

5 In a medium bowl, combine flour, baking soda, and salt.

6 In another bowl, beat together butter, sugar, Stevia, and vanilla extract until creamy. Add flour mixture, and beat again.

7 Add beet mixture and melted chocolate, and beat until well mixed. Beat in egg.

8 Spoon batter into 12 prepared muffin tins, filling about ⅔ full. Bake for about 20 minutes. Cool on wire rack.

PER SERVING (1 cupcake)

197 Calories	9g Sugar
8g Fat (4g sat)	2g Dietary Fiber
5g Protein	28mg Cholesterol
28g Carbohydrates	218mg Sodium

Hazelnut Chocolate Chip Biscotti

Makes about 24 biscotti

1 cup roasted and finely chopped hazelnuts

1¼ cups whole-wheat pastry flour

1½ teaspoons baking powder

½ tablespoon cinnamon

¼ teaspoon nutmeg

¼ teaspoon salt

¼ cup unsalted butter, softened

½ cup sugar

½ teaspoon vanilla extract

1 large egg

¼ cup semisweet mini chocolate chips

1 Preheat oven to 350°.

2 Stir together hazelnuts, flour, baking powder, cinnamon, nutmeg, and salt; set aside.

3 Cream butter and sugar together in mixing bowl with electric beaters until light and fluffy. Beat in vanilla, then egg.

4 Mix dry ingredients into butter mixture. Stir in chocolate chips.

5 On a parchment-lined baking pan, form dough into a log roughly 3 inches wide by 8 inches long. Bake for about 16 minutes.

6 Remove from oven, and cool 10 minutes.

7 Reduce oven to 300°. Cut dough log diagonally into ¼-inch thick slices.

8 Return to oven for another 15–20 minutes, turning cookies over halfway through baking. Cool on pan for 10 minutes, then transfer to rack and allow to cool completely.

PER SERVING (1 biscotti)

67 Calories	3.5g Sugar
4g Fat (2g sat)	1g Dietary Fiber
1g Protein	9mg Cholesterol
8g Carbohydrates	37mg Sodium

Dr. James Rouse

Pistachio Meringues

Makes about 24 meringues

Pistachios are rich in cholesterol-lowering phytosterols (plant-based chemicals that may help lower blood cholesterol and lower your risk for some cancers, too). A 2011 study published in the journal, Diabetes Care, suggested that nuts, including pistachios, are a healthy food choice for people with type 2 diabetes, helping to improve control of blood sugar and cholesterol levels.

1¼ cups shelled unsalted pistachio nuts

½ teaspoon ground cinnamon

4 large egg whites

¼ teaspoon cream of tartar

1 teaspoon Stevia

⅓ cup sugar

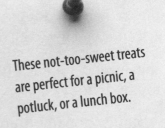

These not-too-sweet treats are perfect for a picnic, a potluck, or a lunch box.

1 Preheat oven to 225°. Prepare nonstick baking sheets (or cookie sheets) by lining them with parchment paper.

2 Shell pistachio nuts, and process them in food processor or coffee grinder until they reach a mealy consistency (before turning into pistachio "butter"). Add to a small bowl, and toss with cinnamon.

3 In a medium bowl, combine egg whites with cream of tartar, and beat with an electric mixture until soft peaks form.

4 Add Stevia and sugar, and continue to beat until egg whites form stiff peaks. Fold in pistachio nut mixture.

5 Drop by heaping tablespoons onto prepared parchment, leaving about an inch between each meringue. Bake for about 45 minutes.

6 Cool on baking sheet for 10 minutes, and then transfer to wire rack.

PER SERVING (2 meringues)

53 Calories	3.25g Sugar
3g Fat (trace sat)	1g Dietary Fiber
2g Protein	0mg Cholesterol
5g Carbohydrates	10mg Sodium

Whole-Wheat Rugelach

Makes 36 pieces

The name rugelach stems from Yiddish and can be translated as "little twists." Making rugelach has been a holiday tradition in our house for years and stems back to Debra's childhood. Our kids look forward to receiving a care package of rugelach from Nana every summer when they're away for camp. We've cut some of the fat and sugar out of a traditional recipe, but these still taste amazing. Sometimes we'll use different flavored jams, and occasionally we've been known to add a few mini chocolate chips.

2 cups whole-wheat pastry flour, or Gluten-Free Flour Mixture, page 44

½ teaspoon baking powder

8 ounces Neufchâtel cream cheese, room temperature

4 tablespoons unsalted butter, softened

¼ cup Greek-style yogurt

¼ cup sugar, divided

8 ounces unsalted butter, softened

2 tablespoons apricot preserves

¼ cup finely chopped walnuts

½ teaspoon cinnamon

1 teaspoon sugar

1 egg, beaten, for egg wash

1 Sift together the flour and baking powder. Set aside.

2 Blend the cream cheese, butter, yogurt, and 2 tablespoons sugar until smooth and creamy. Blend in the flour until combined.

3 Wrap the dough in plastic, or place in a sealable glass container. Chill for 2 hours.

4 Divide the dough into 3 balls. On a lightly floured surface, roll 1 dough ball at a time (refrigerating remaining dough) into a ¼-inch-thick and 9-inch-wide circle.

5 Spread a thin layer of apricot preserves onto the top of dough.

6 Combine walnuts, cinnamon, and sugar in a small bowl. Lightly sprinkle about 1½ tablespoons walnut mixture on top of apricot layer. Press lightly into dough.

7 Cut the dough into 12 triangles. Roll each piece from the wide end to the pointed tip. Place on paper-lined sheet pans; brush with egg wash. Repeat with other 2 balls of dough.

8 Bake at 375° until lightly golden, 12–14 minutes.

PER SERVING (1 cookie)

113 Calories	2.5g Sugar
9g Fat (5g sat)	1g Dietary Fiber
2g Protein	22mg Cholesterol
8g Carbohydrates	34mg Sodium

Kale Brownies

We wanted to incorporate kale into one of our desserts, and we think we did a pretty decent job. You really don't "taste" the kale in this recipe, although you can see a few green specks in the finished product. Try it with Chocolate Cashew Frosting (page 185). Your friends may really think you've gone off the hippie deep end, but you can tell them about all the wonderful qualities they are getting, including vitamins, minerals, fiber, antioxidants, and protein...not your typical story when it comes to eating cake.

2 cups chopped kale

2 tablespoons butter, softened

¼ cup packed brown sugar

1½ teaspoons vanilla extract

2 medium eggs

1 cup oat flour

¾ teaspoon baking powder

¼ cup cocoa powder

3 ounces bittersweet chocolate, melted

1 Steam chopped kale in small amount of water for about 5 minutes. Drain, and purée in a food processor until smooth.

2 Preheat oven to 350°. Prepare 8x8-inch baking pan by coating with cooking spray or lining with parchment paper.

3 In a medium bowl, combine softened butter with sugar, vanilla extract, and eggs. Beat until creamy.

4 Add flour, baking powder, and cocoa powder, and beat again.

5 Beat in melted chocolate and puréed kale. Spoon batter into prepared pan. Bake for 30 minutes or until cooked through.

6 Cool. To serve, cut into 12 squares.

PER SERVING (1 brownie)

175 Calories	7g Sugar
9g Fat (4g sat)	3g Dietary Fiber
5g Protein	41mg Cholesterol
22g Carbohydrates	73mg Sodium

Black Bean Brownies

Black Bean Brownies

Makes 16 servings

¾ cup cooked black beans

½ cup canola oil or melted butter

2 eggs

¼ cup unsweetened cocoa powder

½ cup sugar

1 teaspoon instant coffee

1 teaspoon vanilla extract

½ cup whole-wheat pastry flour, or Gluten-Free Flour Mixture, page 44

½ teaspoon baking powder

¼ teaspoon salt

½ cup semisweet chocolate chips, divided

¼ cup chopped walnuts

1 Preheat the oven to 350°. Prepare a 9x9-inch square baking pan by coating lightly with cooking oil spray. Lining the bottom with parchment paper will also make the brownies much easier to remove.

2 In a food processor fitted with the S blade, purée the black beans, oil, eggs, cocoa powder, sugar, coffee, and vanilla.

3 Pulse in the flour, baking powder, and salt. Scrape down the sides, if necessary.

4 Melt ¼ cup of the chocolate chips (using a double-boiler, or in the microwave in a glass bowl).

5 Add bean mixture to a medium bowl, and stir in melted chocolate. Stir in the remaining chocolate chips and chopped walnuts.

6 Scoop brownie mixture into prepared baking pan. Bake for 25–30 minutes.

7 Allow to cool for at least 20 minutes. To serve, cut into 16 squares.

PER SERVING (1 brownie)

159 Calories	7.125g Sugar
10g Fat (2g sat)	2g Dietary Fiber
3g Protein	27mg Cholesterol
15g Carbohydrates	58mg Sodium

Quinoa Confetti Cookies

Makes 36 cookies

½ cup unsalted butter, softened

2 eggs

½ cup raw sugar

1 teaspoon vanilla

1 cup brown rice flour (or whole-wheat pastry flour)

1 cup rolled oats

1 cup cooked quinoa, cooled

1 teaspoon baking soda

1 teaspoon ground cinnamon

¼ cup chopped organic dried cranberries

¼ cup chopped walnuts

¼ cup chopped currants

¼ cup miniature semisweet chocolate chips

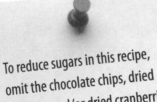

To reduce sugars in this recipe, omit the chocolate chips, dried currants, and/or dried cranberries. We would first omit the chocolate chips, since the dried fruit offer fiber and antioxidants.

1 In a large bowl, cream together butter, eggs, sugar, and vanilla.

2 In another bowl, combine flour, oats, cooked quinoa, baking soda, and ground cinnamon. Stir gently until well mixed.

3 Add flour mixture to wet mixture, and stir or blend until mixed.

4 Stir or gently blend in cranberries, walnuts, currants, and chocolate chips.

5 Cover, and refrigerate cookie dough for about an hour.

6 Preheat oven to 375°. Prepare a large cookie sheet by lining it with parchment paper.

7 Place dough on the cookie sheet by the heaping tablespoon, about 2 inches apart.

8 Bake on middle rack for about 11 minutes. Cookies should just be beginning to brown lightly on top.

9 Remove from oven, and let cool for about 3 minutes, and then carefully move cookies to wire rack to finish cooling.

PER SERVING (1 cookie)

82 Calories	5.8g Sugar
4g Fat (2g sat)	1g Dietary Fiber
2g Protein	19mg Cholesterol
10g Carbohydrates	96mg Sodium

Flourless Peanut Butter Cookies

These cookies are our version of a snickerdoodle cookie, which traditionally is just a sugar cookie with more sugar and cinnamon sprinkled on top.

2 medium eggs

1 teaspoon vanilla extract

1 cup peanut butter

⅓ cup sugar

½ teaspoon cinnamon

½ teaspoon baking powder

½ teaspoon baking soda

1 Preheat oven to 350°. Prepare baking sheet by lining with parchment paper.

2 Add eggs to a medium bowl, and beat with an electric beater for 2 minutes.

3 Add vanilla extract, peanut butter, and sugar, and beat another minute.

4 Add cinnamon, baking powder, and baking soda, and beat until well mixed.

5 Drop by the tablespoon onto prepared baking sheet, and press down with fork. Bake 10 minutes.

6 Allow to cool for a few minutes, then remove to wire rack to finish cooling.

PER SERVING (1 cookie)

163 Calories	5.5g Sugar
12g Fat (2g sat)	1g Dietary Fiber
6g Protein	35mg Cholesterol
10g Carbohydrates	185mg Sodium

Spicy Fruit Salad

Makes 4 servings

1 cup hulled and diced strawberries

1 cup blueberries

1 cup blackberries

1 medium papaya, seeded, peeled, and diced

1 teaspoon fresh lime juice

½ teaspoon seeded and minced jalapeño pepper

1 tablespoon minced mint

1 tablespoon honey

1 Mix fruit in large mixing bowl.

2 In a separate bowl, mix lime juice, jalapeño, mint, and honey. Add to fruit, and toss gently.

PER SERVING

97 Calories	16.5g Sugar
1g Fat	5g Dietary Fiber
1g Protein	0mg Cholesterol
24g Carbohydrates	5mg Sodium

Maple Cream Sauce

Makes 1 cup (4 servings)

A sneaky way to get a little extra protein where you'd least expect it.

1 cup low-fat cottage cheese

1 teaspoon Stevia

½ teaspoon maple extract

½ teaspoon vanilla extract

1 Purée all ingredients together in a blender or food processor.

2 Place in small glass bowl, cover, and refrigerate for at least 30 minutes.

3 This is delicious on top of fruit salad, pies, crisps, breads, and cakes.

PER SERVING (¼ cup)

55 Calories	2.5g Sugar
1g Fat (trace sat)	0g Dietary Fiber
7g Protein	2mg Cholesterol
6g Carbohydrates	230mg Sodium

Dr. James Rouse

Optimum Wellness Tips for Your Metabolic Best

1 Sleep well to be well. Feel great, improve blood sugar, and lose weight!

Be sure to get a good night's sleep. Lack of sleep puts people at a greater risk for obesity and diabetes, as poor, sporadic, and irregular sleep raise blood sugar levels and slow metabolism. Set your intention and your goals to support a great night's sleep. Here's how: Get to bed at the same time each night. Wind down by reading an inspirational book, doing relaxing yoga, or connecting with loved ones rather than the TV or news. Remember, a great night's sleep is not a luxury, it's an essential part of a healthy life and optimum well-being!

2 Change your focus to foods that are good for you, rather than focusing on what you should not eat.

To create new, life- and health-affirming habits, put your focus on what you desire (i.e. more energy, greater vitality, stronger self-confidence, and self-love). Connect eating healthy with the things you want more of in your life. Your body, mind, and spirit are inspired by going for greatness, not by avoiding things. Shift your focus to abundance rather than scarcity, and thrive!

3 Fiber rocks!

One key strategy for living well with diabetes is to get your daily fiber intake; for men 30 grams, for women 25 grams. Fiber not only helps with the healthy management of blood sugar, it also helps with fighting systemic inflammation. Inflammation can lead to a variety of health challenges, from heart disease to many types of cancer, as well as type 2 diabetes. Set your intention and the table to cover your daily fiber needs, and know that you are on your way to healthier blood sugar and overall well-being.

"Increased consumption of vegetables, whole grains, and soluble and insoluble fiber is associated with improved glucose metabolism in both diabetic and nondiabetic individuals. Improvements in insulin sensitivity and glucose homeostasis were more evident in participants following a plant-based diet compared with other commonly used diets." (Wolfram T & Ismail-Beigi F: Efficacy of high-fiber diets in the management of type 2 diabetes mellitus. Endocr Pract. 2011 Jan-Feb;17(1):132-42.)

4 Keep your motivation alive!

Long-term motivation is built by putting your focus on "intrinsic" factors: for example, eating well and exercising is good for my loved ones to witness; or doing it because you desire to be a positive presence in the world. These types of motivating factors are more powerful long-term than doing it to look good, to attain a certain weight, etc. Motivation is an "inside job!"

5 The SAD (Standard American Diet) needs an upgrade.

Most of us are overfed and undernourished. Empty calories drive hunger. Shift your focus to nutrient-dense, delicious, and healthy foods, and you will bump up your satisfaction and your energy. Be mindful at each meal to eat with intention to eat for energy, health, and enjoyment. Think about feeding your mind and heart rather than your emotions, and watch your life thrive!

6 Stress less, eat less, weigh less.

When you are feeling stressed and wanting to eat (everything in sight), give yourself a time out. Stop everything, and simply and slowly breathe from your belly. This will help lower stress hormones and cravings for sweets. Take a lap before you enter the kitchen headed straight for the fridge…or do a few jumping jacks, chase the kids, or your spouse or dog. Any and all movement helps to lower stress and bring you back to balance.

7 Integrity is making good on your good intentions.

You build your self-confidence and your trust by keeping your word and following through. Living well is a lifestyle that is built every moment of your life by simply following through on your good intentions—doing what you know is right and being a force for goodness in thought and in your actions. Live your "A game" and live very well!

8 Low-glycemic carbs that are rich in fiber are good for your blood sugar, your belly, and your brain.

They help promote healthy cholesterol and healthy blood flow to your brain. Choose vegetables, fruits, whole grains, beans, and legumes.

9 Exercise only on the days that you eat.

Not exercising is like taking a "depressant" medication for your mood and your metabolism. Choose to move every day to help keep your hormonal harmony in check, improve insulin and blood sugar levels, and to boost your memory, your mood, and your smile factor. Motion creates positive emotion!

10 Eat fat from fish.

Choose to get your heart-healthy omega-3 oils from fish, nuts, and seeds. Omega-3 oils also help to lower inflammation and aid in heart health and help to lower the risk for many chronic diseases. The American Heart Association suggests that all of us consume healthy omega-3 oils.

11 Whey in on protein.

Adding whey protein powder to orange juice, milk, oatmeal, yogurt, and creamy soups is a simple way to increase the protein in your diet. Whey protein helps to improve insulin sensitivity and can help with bringing greater balance to your blood sugar.

12 Get your kindness on and thrive!

Extend an unexpected kindness to a stranger or someone you know—it can help with supporting both your physiology, happiness, and fulfillment.

13 Practice the empowering art of "BUT" reduction.

Anytime you are desiring to make a positive change in your daily wellness practices and you feel a BUT coming on to keep you from making the step, reduce that BUT and keep moving forward to grow and become your best self!

14 Eat a "rainbow" of life-giving and health-affirming antioxidants .

Diabetes can have a negative effect on many systems and tissues. One powerful way to protect yourself is to eat from a colorful variety of fruits and vegetables. These superfoods can help you to thrive and fight accelerated aging! Rock your rainbow today!

15 Take a TV time out, or take a weekly media fast.

Your body, mind, and spirit will thrive without TV, the news, or other energy and time stealers. Use that time to exercise, cook healthy foods for friends, or do something that stretches your comfort zone and grow! Turn off the TV, and turn on your creativity!

16 Go nuts!

Nuts are a healthy source of heart-healthy fats and blood sugar balancing fiber. Those who snack regularly on nuts tend to be more successful with weight loss and weight management.

17 Are you a time-crunched exerciser?

To get more metabolism out of each breath simply change speeds while you excercise. You will increase your metabolism and endurance in less time.

18 Go green.

Diabetics tend to have lower levels of the very important and powerful antioxidant glutathione. Healthy levels of glutathione are associated with greater overall vitality, health, and longevity. You can build glutathione by enjoying avocados, grapefruit, spinach, and other dark green leafy vegetables.

19 Look on the bright side!

Giving yourself a "check up from the neck up" is good medicine. Optimists have lower inflammation, healthier hearts, and tend to live longer. Join the optimists club today!

20 Be a morning mover.

Exercising in the morning helps you to sleep deeper at night. Deep sleep is the stage where we truly repair, rejuvenate, and recover.

About the Authors

Dr. James Rouse

"Energizing" isn't a word that leaps to mind when describing a visit with your doctor. But Dr. James Rouse isn't your average doc. He's a man affectionately referred to by colleagues as "superhuman." A naturopathic doctor, Ironman triathlete, QVC Network Wellness Specialist, entrepreneur, certified yoga instructor, wellness magazine founder, international speaker, author, radio talk show host, and television personality—Dr. James does it all.

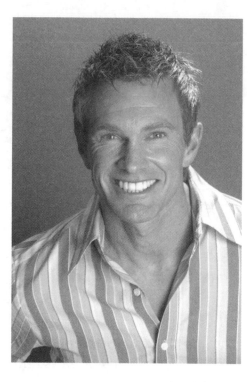

Dr. Debra Rouse

Dr. Debra Rouse is a naturopathic doctor and fitness enthusiast with a passion for creating healthy food. She is the cofounder and co-creator, along with Dr. James, of the Optimum Wellness™ media programs. Dr. Debra is dedicated to educating and inspiring others to take charge of their health.

Index

Dr. James Rouse

INDEX

Dr. James Rouse